You're God's Girl!

A DEVOTIONAL FOR TWEENS

WYNTER PITTS

HARVEST HOUSE PUBLISHERS
EUGENE, OREGON

YOU'RE GOD'S GIRL!

Copyright © 2016 Wynter Pitts
Published by Harvest House Publishers
Eugene, Oregon 97402
www.harvesthousepublishers.com

ISBN 978-0-7369-6736-5 (pbk.)
ISBN 978-0-7369-6737-2 (eBook)

Library of Congress Cataloging-in-Publication Data
Names: Pitts, Wynter, author.
Title: You're God's girl! / Wynter Pitts.
Description: Eugene, Oregon : Harvest House Publishers, 2016.
Identifiers: LCCN 2015051271 (print) | LCCN 2016015634 (ebook) | ISBN
    9780736967365 (pbk.) | ISBN 9780736967372 (eBook)
Subjects: LCSH: Girls—Religious life.
Classification: LCC BV4551.3 .P583 2016 (print) | LCC BV4551.3 (ebook) | DDC
    248.8/2—dc23
LC record available at https://lccn.loc.gov/2015051271

Printed in the United States of America

16 17 18 19 20 21 22 23 24 /VP-JC/ 10 9 8 7 6 5 4 3 2

A special note from Alena Pitts,

actress from the movie *War Room*

Hi! My name is Alena!

I'm here to tell you something important.

Here it is: Devotionals are important!

You may be thinking, "Why are they so important?"

Well, I will tell you. Devotionals are important because they are a way for you to spend time with God.

Now, I know there are many ways to spend time with God, but having daily time for God to speak to you is awesome!

So this book—yes, the one you're holding in your hand—is a devotional, and it is for girls just like us.

You will understand all the words in here, you will have fun, and most importantly you'll be encouraged to spend even more time with God. God loves you so much that He sent His Son, Jesus, to die for your sins, so why not spend some time with Him, right?

Have fun reading this book, and remember, God hears you and He wants to have a relationship with you!

 Love,
Alena

Start Here!

Okay, girls. There is something you should know about me and it is a little embarrassing...but I am going to tell you anyway.

I like to talk to myself.

Wait...maybe I should not start by just saying that.

I should say that I like to ask myself questions. Now, that sounds a little better, doesn't it?

Either way, it's true!

Sometimes I ask myself silly and weird questions, like, "What would I look like if I dyed my hair fuchsia?" This is the kind of question that makes me giggle. Just picture me with bright pink hair!

Funny, right?

But sometimes I ask myself really hard questions. For example, here are three pretty difficult questions I have asked myself:

What does God want me to say when I pray?

Why can't I do whatever I want?

Why does anyone else care about what I do?

Sounds like big stuff, doesn't it?

How about you? Do you ever talk to yourself? Or ask yourself hard questions even though you know you can't really give yourself an answer?

I am thinking you said, "Yes!"

I want you to know that asking God questions about Himself, about your life, and about what He is doing is *the best way* for you to get to know Him. But sometimes it can feel like the more you learn, the more questions you have. If you've ever felt like this, then this book is for you!

God wants you to learn about Him, but He also wants you to understand and really know Him. So let's talk and see if we can find answers to some of our really hard questions together. Maybe to some silly ones too.

There may be questions in this book you have never thought about, and that's okay too. I am sure you will learn something new from each of them.

Here is want I want you to do:

1. Grab your Bible, your favorite pen or pencil, and a journal.

2. Choose a time when and a place where you can concentrate on what you are going to read.

3. Pray and ask God to help you to get to know Him better.

4. Choose a devotional and read it.

5. Have fun! Learning about God is not boring because there are so many ways to enjoy your time with Him! At the end of each devotional, you will see an activity. Be sure to take time to do those.

Remember, you are God's daughter, and He wants you to know many wonderful things about yourself and about Him.

Why Does God Take His Name So Seriously?

What do you call your mom?

You may call her many different names when you are trying to get her attention—Mom, Mommy, Mother. However, I bet there are also a few names you would never call her.

For example, my mother's name is Viola. When I was a little girl everyone called her Vi. Everyone except my brother and me, of course! If we needed her help, we would never scream, "Hey, Vi!" I know she would not have liked that very much! Even though Viola is her name, it would be so disrespectful for her children to just walk around screaming "Viola" whenever we felt like it! As a way of showing her respect, when we needed her or just wanted to talk to her, we would call her Mommy.

Think about your teachers at school, your grandparents, or even the pastor of your church. They all expect you to show respect when you call them as well, right?

Do you know who else expects us to show respect when we call Him?

That's right, God does! He definitely wants us to talk to Him whenever we want. However, He does not want us to just scream His name for fun. It's actually very disrespectful to Him.

Did you know the Bible tells us not to use the Lord's name in vain? To use the Lord's name in vain means to say it casually or carelessly, and this warning is actually the third of the Ten Commandments. (You can read all of them for yourself in Exodus 20:2-17). This is God's way of telling us to respect His name. He wants us to show respect when we talk to Him or about Him to others.

I know it is very popular right now to scream things like, "Oh my God!" But God wants you to remember what He says in the Bible: "You shall not misuse the name of the LORD your God, for the LORD will not hold anyone guiltless who misuses his name" (Exodus 20:7).

In other words, respect God's name and let your friends and others know you take God seriously, just like you would any important person!

Dear God, thank You that I know Your name and I can call on You when I need You or when I just feel like talking. Help me to always treat Your name with respect and importance, like it deserves. In Jesus's name, amen.

 God does not want you to use His name disrespectfully, but His name can definitely be celebrated! Here are five ways you can celebrate God's name:

1. Thank Him anytime you want and for anything.
2. Spend time talking to Him.
3. Share what He means to you with your friends.
4. Sing about Him and to Him.
5. Look for Him and His love during your day.

What Is Faith and Why Do I Need It?

Peter walked on water!

I know the world has a lot of Peters in it, but just so we are clear, the one I am talking about was one of Jesus's disciples. And he's the only Peter who has ever walked on water!

Have you ever walked on water?

I didn't think so. Me neither!

If you know anything about water, then it may be hard to believe that Peter actually walked on it. But you can believe it because it is true!

> "Lord, if it's you," Peter replied, "tell me to come to you on the water."
>
> "Come," he said.
>
> Then Peter got down out of the boat, walked on the water and came toward Jesus (Matthew 14:28-29).

So wait! Are you thinking what I am thinking? Not only did Peter walk on water, but it was his idea!

Yes, that is exactly what this Scripture is saying. Peter asked Jesus to help him walk on water, and Jesus did it.

Wow! Can you believe that?

Peter knew a lot about water. The Bible tells us Peter was a fisherman, which means he spent a lot of time in and around water. Yet he was not afraid to ask God to do something impossible. He believed God could do it, even if it didn't make sense to him.

In other words, Peter was a man of crazy faith!

Having faith in God means you believe He can do something even though you don't see Him or even always understand what He may be doing.

So let me ask you a question. Do you have crazy faith? Have you ever asked God to do something impossible?

Did He do it?

It can be a little hard to really understand what it means to have faith, but think about Peter. Having faith means you do not do things based only on what you *know* is possible, but you look to Jesus and believe He can do so much more than what seems possible!

What do you think the other disciples in the boat were thinking when they heard Peter's strange request? They probably thought he was crazy, right? But Peter believed Jesus could help him walk on water even though it is a totally crazy idea. No one walks on water unless God is in control of it!

Always remember, Jesus wants you to have faith in Him. You also have to remember that Jesus wants what is best for you. Even though He may not do exactly what you are asking Him to do, still have faith in Him because He will always do what is best for your life—and you can believe that!

Dear God, thank You for Peter and for all the stories of faith in the Bible. I want to have crazy faith too! Will You help me to not be afraid to ask You for what seems impossible? Help me to trust that You will do what is best for my life even when I do not understand it. In Jesus's name, amen.

 Read Hebrews 11 to see some of the amazing things God did when people had faith in Him. Then make your very own "Faith Book." All you have to do is make a list of things God has done in your life. Whenever you start to have doubts, read your book. I am sure it will not take you long to remember that God will do crazy things in your life when you believe in Him!

Do I Have to Do It?

My favorite socks are pink and fuzzy with little dangling turquoise balls at the top. I just love them so much! I normally wear them with really soft pajama pants and a too-big T-shirt. Wearing these clothes makes me feel super comfortable, and I love to be comfortable!

When are you most comfortable? Maybe you like being dressed up and feel best when your hair is nicely curled and you are wearing your favorite dress. Or maybe you prefer to wear your gym shorts, favorite sneakers, and athletic gear!

If you are not sure, take some time to think about when you feel the most comfortable. It is good to know what you like!

However, you have to be careful, because sometimes being too comfortable can be a bad thing.

Let me explain.

What would happen if I wore my pink fuzzy socks and pajama pants all day while sitting on my couch? I would certainly be comfortable, but I would not be able to do the things I need to get done. Sometimes we have to get away from what makes us the most comfortable to do what we are being asked to do. Think about it— would I go on a job interview wearing my pink fluffy socks?

Everyone has a "comfort zone," and it is normally where they feel safest. But it can also make them not want to try anything new or hard. In the Bible God often asked people to do things that were not very comfortable for them. For example, God called Moses to speak to Pharaoh and be a leader to His people. Moses did not want to do this. He was not comfortable speaking to large crowds. He did not think he spoke well at all. (Maybe you don't like speaking to big groups of people either!) However, God had a big plan for His people. To accomplish that plan Moses needed to do what God commanded, even though it made him uncomfortable. He could trust that God would give him the courage he needed!

Often God asks us to step away from the areas where we are most comfortable so He can use us to do something different. He wants your faith in Him to be more important than being comfortable! If God is asking you to do something, do it. It could be talking to a friend about something hard, joining a sports team, or traveling somewhere far away from home.

Is God asking you to do something different, scary, or strange? Pray and ask Him to help you. Then trust and have faith that He will, and go do it!

Dear God, I know You have special things for me to do. Help me to never be so comfortable doing what feels good to me that I don't want to do what You need me to do. In Jesus's name, amen.

 Read the story of Esther (Hint: Her story is in her book in the Old Testament of the Bible!) and answer the questions below:

1. What was God asking Esther to do?
2. If you were Esther, what would you be most afraid of?
3. What was she afraid of?
4. What did she do to overcome her fears?
5. Is God asking you to do something right now?

How Can I Be Beautiful on the Inside?

Have you ever watched someone build a house?

Yeah, me neither! Well, unless you count those fun homebuyer shows on TV. You know, the ones where they tear down walls, knock out windows, rip up floors, buy new furniture, paint the ceilings, and create an entirely new living space in just three days? Yes, I love those shows!

I am not a homebuilder and I won't even pretend to understand everything it takes. However, I do know building anything takes a lot of materials, supplies, instructions, and especially patience. You need materials like bricks, concrete, nails, and wood if you want your building to last.

What do you think would happen to a house if the builders decided not to use any nails? Or to use plastic where they should use wood? The house might look good for a little while, but eventually the walls would start falling down, right? How awful would that be?

You and I are kind of like new buildings. You may be thinking, "Well, I don't need nails and concrete inside me." But we need different types of supplies. As children of God we want to grow into beautiful, well-designed women, so we need things like honesty, patience, and kindness inside us!

These building supplies—or characteristics—make up what we call our *character*. They are the pieces of our lives that matter the most. Most people do not see them, just like they don't see the nails that hold up a house. But if you want a strong, beautiful character, they must be present. And guess who our builder is?

> Every house is built by someone, but God is the builder of everything (Hebrews 3:4).

God is the builder of everything. That includes you and your character. He created you and knows just how He needs you to look on the inside. If you want to make sure you are full of the characteristics you need, then you have to spend time with Him! Let Him give you what you need to stand strong and beautiful.

Our character is on the inside, but people will definitely notice the difference on the outside. Spending time with God, seeking Him, and asking Him to build you is what makes you beautiful!

Dear God, I want to be strong and beautiful on the outside and on the inside. When people see me, I want them to see You. Will You build my character? Help me to be full of love, joy, peace, patience, kindness, goodness, faithfulness, gentleness, and self-control. In Jesus's name, amen.

Go to Galatians 5:22-23 to find the characteristics God wants to use as He builds you into a strong, beautiful woman.

What Is the Fruit of the Spirit?

The fruit of the Spirit are those characteristics only God can grow in your life. He tells you there is *no* limit on the amount of these building materials in the house of our hearts. He wants to grow you more and more in these areas:

Which fruit am I? ___ ___ ___ ___

1. I am a four-letter word.
2. I live in your heart.
3. I am the way you feel about your family and close friends.
4. The color that represents me most often is red.
5. A popular symbol represents me all over the world.
6. A holiday that celebrates me in the United States comes every February.
7. In Mark 12:30, Jesus tells us the most important commandment is to "_____ the Lord your God with all your heart and with all your soul and with all your mind and with all your strength."
8. He also tells us in Mark 12:31 to "_____ your neighbor as yourself."
9. First Corinthians 13:4-13 tells us a lot about me also. "_____ is patient, _____ is kind. It does not envy, it does not boast, it is not proud" (verse 4).

10. These verses also tell us that "_____ never fails" (verse 8).

Which fruit am I? ___ ___ ___ ___ ___ ___ ___ ___

1. I am an eight-letter word.

2. I help you wait calmly until it is your turn.

3. A famous phrase that talks about me is "_____ is a virtue."

4. I can help you when you are waiting in line, at the doctor's office, or for an answer from your parents.

5. Some words that end with the same sound as me are *balance*, *brilliance*, *distance*, and *science*.

6. Two bigger words that have similar meanings to me are *endurance* and *persistence*.

7. The word that describes someone who shows me is a homonym (a word that only sounds the same) for the name of the person a doctor takes care of.

8. "A hot-tempered person stirs up conflict, but the one who is _____ calms a quarrel" (Proverbs 15:18).

9. First Corinthians 13:4 says, "Love is _____, love is kind."

10. Romans 12:12 tells us to "Be joyful in hope, _____ in affliction, faithful in prayer."

Which fruit am I? ___ ___ ___ ___ ___

1. I am a five-letter word.

2. Some of my synonyms (words that mean exactly or nearly the same) are *calm*, *silence*, and *stillness*.

3. My symbol was popular in the 1960s and 1970s, and it is popular again with girls your age today.

4. You can show another symbol of me with two of your fingers.

5. I am the opposite of war, disagreement, and fighting.

6. A dove with an olive branch is another symbol of me.

7. Some other words that have similar meaning to me are *harmony*, *tranquility*, and *serenity*.

8. A prize is awarded on December 10 of every year to internationally famous people who have promoted me in their life and work.

9. "The _____ of God, which transcends all understanding, will guard your hearts and your minds in Christ Jesus" (Philippians 4:7).

10. "_____ I leave with you; my _____ I give you. I do not give to you as the world gives. Do not let your hearts be troubled and do not be afraid" (John 14:27).

Which fruit am I? ___ ___ ___ ___ ___ ___ ___ ___

1. I am an eight-letter word.

2. I am what is right and fair.

3. I am the opposite of doing and thinking bad or evil things.

4. Some of my synonyms are *integrity*, *kindness*, *honesty*, and *righteousness*.

5. Some of my antonyms (words that mean the opposite) are *badness*, *wickedness*, *immorality*, and *evil*.

6. A popular phrase people use when something happens is "O my _____."

7. In the movie *Annie*, one of the orphan girl characters, July, says, "Oh my _____, Oh my _____!"

8. Another phrase used to show surprise is "_____ gracious!"

9. "Surely your _____ and love will follow me all the days of my life, and I will dwell in the house of the LORD forever" (Psalm 23:6).

10. "What shall I return to the LORD for all his _____ to me?" (Psalm 116:12).

Which fruit am I? ___ ___ ___ ___ ___ ___ ___ ___

1. I am an eight-letter word.

2. When you help others you are showing me.

3. It is a good thing to show acts of _____.

4. When you show me to others, you are also showing respect.

5. My dictionary definition is "showing like for someone or something."

6. Some of my synonyms are *friendliness*, *compassion*, *kindheartedness*, *thoughtfulness*, and *benevolence*.

7. I am one of the most important qualities of being a good friend.

8. *Cruelness*, *meanness*, and *harshness* are three of my antonyms.

9. "With everlasting _____ I will have compassion on you" (Isaiah 54:8).

10. This Bible verse uses my root word (the main part of me). "Love is patient, love is _____. It does not envy, it does not boast, it is not proud" (1 Corinthians 13:4).

Which fruit am I?

_____ _____ _____ _____ _____ _____ _____ _____ _____ _____ _____ _____

1. I am a 12-letter word.

2. *Loyalty*, *dependability*, and *trustworthiness* are three of my synonyms.

3. When you show me, people know they can count on you and believe in you.

4. *Dishonest*, *disloyalty*, and *falseness* are three words that have the opposite meaning.

5. A popular hymn, a Christian song, is about me. It is titled "Great Is Thy _____."

6. Psalm 36:5, also used in a popular Christian song, says, "Your love, LORD, reaches to the heavens, your _____ to the skies."

7. Lamentations 3:22-23 is also used in a popular Christian song. "His compassions never fail. They are new every morning; great is your _____."

8. In a story told in Matthew 25, in verse 23 a master says to his servant, "Well done, good and _____ servant! You have been _____

with a few things; I will put you in charge of many things."

9. "If we confess our sins, he is _____ and just and will forgive us our sins and purify us from all unrighteousness" (1 John 1:9).

10. "A _____ person will be richly blessed, but one eager to get rich will not go unpunished" (Proverbs 28:20).

Which fruit am I?

—— —— —— —— —— —— —— —— ——

1. I am a ten-letter word.

2. You would treat a baby with _____.

3. You would also treat most pets with

   _____.

4. Two of my synonyms are *tenderness* and *softness*.

5. *Roughness* is one of my antonyms.

6. "Let your _____ be evident to all. The Lord is near" (Philippians 4:5).

7. "In your hearts revere Christ as Lord. Always be prepared to give an answer to everyone who asks you to give the reason for the hope that you have. But do this with _____ and respect." (1 Peter 3:15).

8. "As God's chosen people, holy and dearly loved, clothe yourselves with compassion, kindness, humility, _____ and patience" (Colossians 3:12).

9. "Be completely humble and _____; be patient, bearing with one another in love" (Ephesians 4:2).

10. "A _____ answer turns away wrath, but a harsh word stirs up anger" (Proverbs 15:1).

Which fruit am I?
__ __ __ __ - __ __ __ __ __ __ __

1. I am an 11-letter word.
2. I am a hyphenated word.
3. I help you make good choices when it is difficult.
4. If you don't use me at school, you may get into trouble.
5. Through discipline and reward, parents teach this to their children.
6. *Self-discipline* and *restraint* are two of my synonyms.
7. Words like *excess* and *indulgence* have the opposite meaning.
8. A person who is tempted but resists temptation is showing _____-_____.
9. "Better a patient person than a warrior, one with _____-_____ than one who takes a city" (Proverbs 16:32).
10. "Make every effort to add to your faith goodness; and to goodness, knowledge; and to knowledge, _____-_____; and to_____-_____, perseverance; and to perseverance, godliness; and to godliness, mutual affection; and to mutual affection, love" (2 Peter 1:5-7).

Which fruit am I? ___ ___ ___

1. I am a 3-letter word.

2. I can make your heart smile no matter what is going on.

3. I might make you laugh or giggle.

4. I am a feeling similar to happy, but even better!

5. I am contagious, and if you show me around others they may start to feel me too.

6. Some of my synonyms are *delight*, *pleasure*, *enjoyment*, and *elation*.

7. There is a Christmas carol titled "_____ to the World."

8. Psalm 100:1 tells us to "Shout for _____ to the LORD, all the earth."

9. In Nehemiah 8:10, Nehemiah says, "The _____ of the LORD is your strength."

10. In John 15, Jesus tells us to keep His commandments, and in verse 11 He says, "I have told you this so that my _____ may be in you and that your _____ may be complete."

How Do I Speak "Love"?

Did you know millions of creatures live on the earth and in the ocean? They each have special things about them and they are different from each other in many ways.

God created every living thing. Every plant, every animal, every person. Including you!

Out of the millions of other living things, one reason people are so special is that we have languages and we use words to communicate with each other. Think about it. Can any other living things open their mouths and form sentences?

No!

Yes, some animals make sounds, but God gave people more than sounds. He gave us a vocabulary and so many different words to express how we feel and what we think.

With words comes a pretty big responsibility. The Bible says words are powerful. Proverbs 18:21 says, "The tongue has the power of life and death, and those who love it will eat its fruit." How you use your words is a big deal. You are in charge of what you say to other people and you are also responsible for what happens with the words you use.

I know it may be hard to speak kindly to your little sister or brother after they've ripped a page from your favorite book. I know it is not easy to be kind to the girl in class who always takes your pencil. But with God's help, you can do it. Kind words make you feel special and they help the people around you feel loved.

Have you hurt someone with your words? Today, find them and use the words "I am sorry" to help make it better!

Dear God, thank You for trusting me with words. I know You did not have to give me so many words to express how I am feeling, but I am thankful You did. Sometimes it is hard to speak kindly, but I pray that You will help me! Help me use my words to show others Your love. In Jesus's name, amen.

Use this space to make a list of words that hurt. Whenever you feel like using one of the words from your list, remember how much they can hurt and erase them from your vocabulary!

Does the Fruit of the Spirit Have Anything to Do with Apples?

I t was the middle of the morning, after breakfast but before lunch, when my stomach began to make funny noises. I knew exactly what that meant. I was hungry!

There on the table, right in front of me, was just what I needed: a perfectly round and brightly colored apple. It looked delicious and it seemed to be waiting for me. My mouth began watering just thinking about taking a big, crunchy, juicy bite. It was the perfect solution to my hunger problem!

I reached out and grabbed it. I pulled it close to my mouth, opened wide, and chomped down. However, within seconds, I tossed the apple back onto the table. That beautiful piece of fruit was the worst thing I had ever tasted. It was rotten on the inside and there was nothing delicious or sweet about it!

A piece of fruit can taste so good and is good for you. But if it's rotten on the inside, it loses its yummy flavor and no one will want to eat it. Regardless of how pretty it is, a rotten piece of fruit is worthless.

Have you ever noticed that the Bible talks about fruit a lot? God even describes what our character should be like by using the words *fruit of the Spirit*. "The fruit of the Spirit is love, joy, peace, forbearance, kindness, goodness, faithfulness, gentleness and self-control" (Galatians 5:22-23).

Character is a word that describes how you think, how you

act, and how you treat other people. It's the way you've developed your personality.

It may sound weird, but God wants us to taste good! He wants us to be the love, joy, peace, forbearance, kindness, goodness, faithfulness, gentleness, and self-control others will see in us and want to try.

God created each of us beautiful on the outside, and He wants our insides to be full of His goodness for others to enjoy. When we are impatient, mean, or evil, then we are growing rotten fruit and other people will not want to be around us or have any of it.

Ask God to help you to grow juicy and tasty fruit on the inside! How can you show one or more of the fruit of the Spirit with your friends and family?

. . . .

Dear God, thank You for showing me what my insides should look like. Please help me to be full of the juicy and tasty fruit of Your Spirit so other people might taste and see You in me! In Jesus's name, amen.

5 Ways to Grow Good Fruit!

Be joyful: Read Philippians 4:4.
Speak love: Read Ephesians 4:29.
Work hard: Read Proverbs 13:4.
Be an example: Read 1 Timothy 4:12.
Stay focused: Read Philippians 4:8.

Am I a Light?

Do you have a night-light in your bedroom or in a hallway close by? A night-light makes you feel safe by helping you to see what is happening around you. It keeps you from hurting yourself. If you have to get up in the middle of the night to go to the bathroom or go talk to your mom, a light will keep you from stepping on a small toy or falling over something.

A night-light in a dark room can also save your mom or dad or someone else from pain when they walk in. Yes, your night-light helps you, but it also helps others. When it is on, you have no choice but to share it. No matter how hard you try, you just cannot keep a light to yourself. Others can see a light shining in your room!

Matthew 5:14 says, "You are the light of the world. A town built on a hill cannot be hidden." Without knowing God, the world is dark, just like a room with no light. People who do not know Him can't see clearly. Just like a night-light, with Jesus in you, your life should shine so bright that it helps those around you feel safe and see in the dark!

It could be the way you smile, the way you help your neighbor, or the way you act when things do not go the way you want them to. When you show Jesus in you, others see how good God really is. So go shine bright today!

Dear God, I know that without You the world can be dark, so thank You for helping me to see. Please help me show Jesus in everything I think, do, and say today. In Jesus's name, amen.

 Can you think of one person who needs to see God's light? Brainstorm a few ways you can shine on them today. Here are a few examples: Help clean up without being asked, pray with a friend, help a sibling with their homework, or smile at someone who seems sad. Write about what you did and how it made you feel. Don't forget to thank God for helping you shine!

Am I Part of God's Story?

I love to hear a good story! Do you? In a book, on a television screen, or even over the phone?

I just get so excited when a friend calls and says, "I have something to tell you!" I love to know the details of all the fun things happening in their life.

Of course, sometimes stories can be mean, negative, and more gossip than truth. Those are not the stories I am talking about. As God's children, we need to make sure we are not a part of those stories. But I bet you already know that, right?

Do you realize your life and all the details in it make up the pieces of a story?

They do! Think about the day you were born. I know you don't remember it, but that would be the first page. Your first day of kindergarten, the day you lost your first tooth, and the day you met your best friend would probably be everyone's favorite chapters.

You may not think your story is as interesting or fun as the stories you watch on TV or read in a book, but it is way more important.

Guess who is writing it?

God is!

There are no better stories than the ones written by God. Way back when He first created the world, He knew the part of His story He wanted your life to be in.

Ephesians 2:10 says, "We are God's handiwork, created in Christ Jesus to do good works, which God prepared in advance for us to do." This means God created you because He has something to show others, and it is good! Your life's story is actually part of something way bigger—He wants to use your life to tell His story.

And every detail matters. There is nothing about you that God does not plan to use to show someone else His love.

Just think about your favorite book or story and the characters in it. What would happen if one of them decided they did not want to do what the author planned for them? The story would be completely different and it would affect all the other characters, right? If Goldilocks decided not to eat the porridge or the wolf decided not to blow down the house—what a disaster that would be for the story!

Well, the same is true for God's story and His children. How you choose to live your life matters—not just for you but for those around you. So when you are making decisions, pray and ask God to show you His plans!

Dear God, thank You for making me a part of Your story. Help me to stay close to You so I know what You have planned for my life. I am excited to live each day for You and to be a part of all the wonderful things You do. In Jesus's name, amen.

Let's title your chapter in God's story! Your chapter is special to Him and those around you. What would you call it? Think creatively and ask God to help you with it.

The title of my chapter would be

_____

because

_____

_____.

Why Do I Have to Do It?

Let's play a game!

I want you to choose your answer. There is no loser in this game and you do not have to tell anyone your answer.

What would you do if you saw a sock or a piece of trash on the floor in your house? It is not your sock and you did not leave the trash.

1. Walk by it and leave it there, waiting for the person who left it to pick it up.

2. Pick it up.

3. Find the person it belongs to and tell them they need to clean up after themselves.

4. Pick it up and find the person who left it so you can tell them what you did.

This happens in my house all the time! Maybe it happens in yours too. It can be really frustrating to see someone made a mess and didn't clean it up, right?

But have you ever made a mess and forgotten to clean it up?

Let's pretend you had a really busy week at school and you have been a little messier than normal. How special would you feel if your mom or little brother decided to clean your room for you to help you out?

I'm thinking you would love that, am I right?

Taking care of the people and things around us is a wonderful way to show God's love! God takes care of us and cleans up our messes all the time. He also protects us and gives us people to love, and we certainly cannot forget that He died for us!

Remember what John 3:16 says. "God so loved the world that he gave his one and only Son, that whoever believes in him shall not perish but have eternal life." How awful would our lives be if Jesus decided He did not want to be responsible for the messes we make? There would be no more forgiveness and no more grace, and we would always get what we deserved.

That's scary!

We need Jesus's help. Remember that being helpful to others is just one small way we say thank you to Him and remind ourselves that we need the very same help!

Dear God, thank You for taking care of my mess! Help me to look for ways to help those around me. I know I need them, and sometimes they need me too. Help me to show Your love whenever I have the chance. In Jesus's name, amen.

 Here are a few ways to get your brain thinking about how you can help those around you. Could you do one of these chores without even being asked?

- Clean your parents' bathroom.
- Pick up your brother's mess.
- Take out the trash.
- Mop the kitchen floor.
- Vacuum the entire house.
- Mow the lawn.
- Wash dirty clothes.
- Fold clean laundry.

Will God Really Give Me Whatever I Want?

One verse in the Bible can be pretty confusing. Well, actually many verses in the Bible can be confusing. That's why we must always ask God to help us understand what He wants to teach us.

John 15:7 says, "If you remain in me and my words remain in you, ask whatever you wish, and it will be done for you."

That means you can pray for whatever you want and God will give it to you, right?

Unfortunately, that is not completely true.

Let me explain.

God wants a relationship with you. He wants you to know Him. Not just to ask Him for things when you need or want them, but to talk to Him all the time! In this verse, Jesus is telling His disciples—and you—to stay close to Him. He wants to give you what's best, but you have to stay close to Him to know what those things are.

Try thinking about it this way: If you went shopping for your best friend, would you be able to pick out an outfit she'd love? I think you probably would. You spend so much time with her and you know her so well! You would never want to buy her something she'd hate or never wear, right?

This is exactly how God wants us to be with Him. He knows us so well that He knows what's best for us. And He wants us to know Him so well that we would never want anything He wouldn't want us to have.

Spend time getting to know God. When you pray, don't get so busy asking for the things you want that you miss knowing the things God actually wants to give you!

Dear God, it makes me so happy to know I can ask You for anything! I want what You know is best for me. Will You help me to spend time getting to know You better? I know You only want what is best for my life and I am grateful that You take care of me. In Jesus's name, amen.

 What do you want most from God? Why? Now, read Matthew 22:37-39. What does God want most for you?

How Could God Know What It Is Like to Be Me?

Have you ever realized that when Jesus came to earth, He really did come as an actual person? The Bible says God became flesh and walked the earth as a man! He was both God and man.

Now, think about that for a moment. If Jesus became a person, that means He had a body just like you and me. While He was on earth, He went through the same stages of life as every other person. He was a baby, a little boy, a teenager, and a grown-up!

That means Jesus knows what it feels like to be hungry, silly, sleepy, hot, and cold. Jesus had friends and enemies. He even had to do scary things and make really hard choices. This means Jesus knows what it is like to be you!

Hebrews 4:15 says, "We do not have a high priest who is unable to empathize with our weaknesses, but we have one who has been tempted in every way, just as we are—yet he did not sin." This means Jesus gets you! He understands the human emotions you feel over the situations you have to face because He has felt the exact same emotions. However, because Jesus is God's Son, He did not sin, not even when He was human!

So the next time you are going through something, anything, pray about it. Jesus wants you to talk to Him because He understands, and He has the answers and tools you need. He wants to help you make the best choices for your life!

Dear God, it feels so good to know You not only hear my prayers but that You understand me. Sometimes when I am going through difficult situations, it feels like no one gets me. Thank You for reminding me that I do not have to deal with difficult times alone. In Jesus's name, amen.

 Now that you know Jesus was both God and human—both divine and a person just like you—let's see if you can answer the following questions.

Circle "true" or "false." (Hint: The verses listed will help you.)

Jesus never cried.
John 11:35
True   False

Jesus needed rest.
Mark 4:35-40
True   False

Jesus could not eat.
Matthew 9:9-11
True   False

People were always nice to Jesus.
Matthew 27:27-31
True   False

Satan tried to get Jesus to do something wrong.
Matthew 4:1-11
True   False

What Should I Say to God When I Pray?

When I was a little girl, I would watch my grandmother pray for what seemed like forever. She liked to pray in the morning, so breakfast would have to wait and my stomach would growl until she was finished. This was a little upsetting because we all know how hungry we can be when we first wake up!

She would sit on her bed, her Bible in her hands, wearing her favorite pair of tiny purple framed glasses. With tears streaming down her cheeks, she would talk to God as if He were sitting on the bed next to her. Sometimes she was so loud that my brother and I would think she had a friend over visiting! But she never did. When we peeked into her room, she was the only person sitting there.

My grandmother's conversations with God made me really curious. Why was she talking to Him, and did He ever talk back?

Prayer. I had so many questions about it. I had things I wanted to talk to God about, too, but I could never get my prayers to last for more than a few seconds...a minute, maybe, if it was a little closer to Christmas or my birthday!

I figured that, just maybe, the older I got the more I would have to say to Him. Well, I only became more frustrated. Honestly, sometimes I wondered why I should bother praying at all. In my mind I would say, "God never seems to do or give me what I am asking for anyway!"

What about you? Do you pray? Do you always know what to say? Does God answer your prayers?

If you are anything like I was as a girl, you probably pray over your pancakes just before you take the first bite. You may even pray, "God, will You help me, please?" while sitting in the middle of your history test trying to remember the thirteenth president of the United States! And you probably pray at the end of each day, thanking God for keeping you safe, right before you close your eyes.

Zzzzzzzzzzzzzz!

But maybe you are nothing like I was and you don't know much about praying at all! Actually, you think the whole idea of what sounds like talking to yourself is a bit weird. I can relate to that too.

Whatever you think about prayer, know that God loves it when you talk to Him. And do you know what else? He loves to talk to His children! Not just His adult children but *all* His children, and that includes you.

Prayer is not just about asking God to help us. Prayer is how we build a relationship with God. He wants us to talk to Him and He wants to talk to us.

Dear God, thank You for always being there for me to talk to. Sometimes it feels weird because I cannot see You, but help me to remember that You are with me all the time. Teach me how to pray and how to listen so that I can know You better. In Jesus's name, amen.

Need help knowing how and what to pray? Let's make it simple!

Sometimes prayer seems hard because we think it is supposed to be quiet and boring, but I don't know where we got that silly idea. Remember, God wants to know you and wants you to know Him. So let's spend some time praying. Here are a few easy things to focus on when you pray:

1. **Praise:** Worship God! You get to pick how. Do you want to sing a song to Him? Do you want to dance for Him? Do you want to color or draw a picture for Him? You can express how you feel about God in lots of ways, so be creative!

2. **Thanks:** There is so much you can be thankful for today! What can you think of? Choose one or two things and write them down. You can always go back in your memory to remind yourself what God has done for you.

3. **Others:** Pray for other people. Your mom, dad, brothers, sisters, friends, teachers, pastor. If God brings anyone to your mind, talk about them with God and ask Him to meet their needs.

4. **You:** What do you need help with? Write it all down and talk to God about the needs in your life. Remember, He cares!

5. **Confession:** What are some things you need to ask God to forgive you for? Talking to God about the areas where you didn't do so well will always remind you of how much you need Him. And you can count on God to forgive you and clean you up. Find 1 John 1:9 in your Bible and write it out!

Can God Be My Friend?

Do you know what it means to have a relationship with someone?

The word *relationship* means you are connected to someone for a reason. Think about your relationship with your mom or dad. God connected you with them so you would have someone to take care of you. God gave you teachers to help you learn.

Can you think of a few other people you have a good relationship with? People at school, at church, or even in your family?

You probably didn't feel close to them right away. And you may notice that you are closer to the people you spend the most time with, right? By playing together, sitting next to each other in class, talking to each other, and hanging out, you learn what makes them happy and what makes them sad. You get to know their personality and they get to know yours. Over time you become really good friends!

Do you know that God wants to have a relationship with you too?

Just like the relationships you have with your friends, the more time you spend together with God the more you get to know Him.

The Bible says, "Grow in the grace and knowledge of our Lord and Savior Jesus Christ" (2 Peter 3:18). God wants you to learn all about Him. He wants you to know what makes Him happy and what makes Him sad. Most of all, He wants you to learn all about His love.

Spending time together is a big deal and it is really the only way to get to know someone. How can you spend time getting to know God today?

Ask God to help you to get to know Him better so you can have an awesome relationship with Him!

• •

Dear God, thank You for wanting to have a relationship with me. Help me know how important it is to spend time with You. Teach me about Your love and who You are. I pray that I will know You are my best friend and always look for ways to spend time with You and get to know You better! In Jesus's name, amen.

Does your schedule get really busy? Don't forget to make time to spend alone with God. Sometimes you have to plan a date with Him. Plan ahead for a few special moments with God. Write down the time and place where you're going to meet Him, and write out an agenda. (*Agenda* is just a fancy word for *plan*.) Decide how you will spend your time with Him and think about what you'll talk about.

Time:

Place:

Agenda:

Does God Want Me?

Have you ever been in class at school waiting for your teacher to choose her special helper? Or how about in your Sunday school class, waiting for your leader to select the winner of the Bible verse contest? Maybe you like to play sports. Have you ever waited to be picked by one of the two team captains for the next game of soccer or volleyball or kickball?

In times like these, each second seems to drag on like minutes. So many thoughts can begin running through your mind as you wait in total excitement or fear. You might think, "Am I good enough?" "Do they like me enough?" "If I get picked, will I be able to do what they think I can do?"

Finally, that moment comes and you hear your name called. You don't believe it. At first you don't want to move forward, wanting to be sure that you heard what you thought you heard. You hear the words again in your head and a smile comes over your face. Your heart begins to beat faster. You walk to the front of the classroom or you step out to join the rest of the team that you are a part of now. A joy and confidence comes over you as you realize you have been chosen.

Do you know that God has already chosen you to be a part of His team? You don't have to be nervous, wondering if you have been picked. You can live with confidence and joy, knowing that God wants you! He wants you on His team. He chose you because He has a plan for you, and you are just the one He had in mind!

How does it feel to know that the King of the world wants you?

Dear God, it makes me feel really special to know You chose me. I am excited to see what You are planning for my life. Help me live so others can tell I am on Your team! In Jesus's name, amen.

 If you were a coach, what kind of people would you want on your team? List the characteristics you would like for them to have and explain why those specific characteristics are important for a team.

Am I Enough?

Do you worry about what people think about you or if they even like you? How much time do you spend choosing the perfect outfit to make sure others will love it? Do you worry about the perfect thing to say to make everyone laugh?

It is easy for us to care a lot about what others think of us. Wanting to be liked is very normal. And, honestly, there is nothing wrong with caring about how you look. You should always want to look and feel your best. However, if you put all your energy into trying to make everyone like you, then you may forget to be yourself. You know, the fabulous girl God created you to be!

You will never be able to do enough or be good enough to please everyone. Pleasing everyone is not something God wants you to worry about. Yes, you are expected to treat others kindly and to be considerate always. But you just do not have enough talent, skill, or good looks to make everyone happy! Not because you are not awesome enough, but just because it is impossible to do. And more importantly, pleasing everyone is not what God created you to do.

Instead of working hard and worrying about how to make sure everyone likes you, use your energy to make sure everyone sees God in you. Here are two ways the Bible says you can do that:

Luke 6:31 says, "Do to others as you would have them do to you." And in Matthew 22:39, Jesus instructs you to "Love your neighbor as yourself."

When you show people love and treat them kindly and with respect, you are showing them God. Regardless of how cool your hairstyle is or how unbelievably well you can sing and dance, what matters is how much of God people can see in you!

Dear God, help me to care more about being who You created me to be than what I think other people want me to be. Help me to love others in a way that makes You look good. In Jesus's name, amen.

 Read Luke 6:31 and Matthew 22:39. Make a list of what makes you feel loved. Maybe it is when someone writes you a nice note or saves you a seat. Now look at your list and choose a few of those things to do for someone else!

I Love God, but How Do I Know If I Love Something Else More?

Do you know what an idol is? You may have heard someone in church talk about idols or serving other gods, or you may have read about it in the Bible before. When God gave Moses the Ten Commandments, He was especially careful to warn the people about idols.

Idol is probably not a word you use every day, but it is just something or someone that you make more important than God. An idol can be anyone or anything. If you focus all your attention on money, a television show, or making your friends happy, well, any of those things can become your idol. What you think about or worry about most can be like another god to you.

God knows if you put your attention on other things, you will not be able to focus on what He has done for you. But He is the only one who can give you what you need!

There is nothing wrong with wanting to earn money, watching television, or having friends, but you have to make sure you are not making those things what is most important in your life. God wants to be what's most important in your life, always!

In Exodus 20:3 God told His people, "You shall have no other gods before me." This was the first commandment He gave. Obeying this one helps you follow all the other ones! Your life will be better if you put God first.

Can you think of something or someone you have treated like an idol?

....

Dear God, thank You for being my only God. Help me to not focus all my attention on things that cannot help me and do not bring me closer to You. In Jesus's name, amen.

 Is your relationship with God the most important thing in your life? How do you know? What can you do to make sure you are putting God first?

Does God See Me?

You have probably heard that God is *omniscient*. Well, that is just a big word that means He knows everything. You might have also heard that He is *omnipresent*. Yep, another big word, but it just means God is with you wherever you go. You got it, right?

Let's just say these fancy words are a simple way of saying that God sees and knows everything, including you and me!

It may be easy to believe that He knows everything about you and your life. But God does not just see the things you are doing. Nope. He also sees you on the inside and He knows your heart.

He sees what you feel. He knows what you worry about, what makes your heart happy, what you are afraid of. God knows exactly what you are going through even if you have never told anyone else. He knows when you want to do the right things but you just don't know how, and He even knows when you don't really want to do the right thing at all!

One of my favorite stories in the Bible is in the first chapter of John. This is the part of the Bible when people were just meeting Jesus for the first time. John the Baptist was sent by God to baptize people and tell them to prepare their hearts for the Savior. Jesus would be coming soon, and John wanted to make sure the people were ready to meet Him.

When Jesus arrived John began telling people to follow Him and they began to tell their friends to do the same. One guy, Philip, found his friend Nathanael and told him about Jesus. When Jesus saw Nathanael coming, He said,

"Here truly is an Israelite in whom there is no deceit."

"How do you know me?" Nathanael asked.

Jesus answered, "I saw you while you were still under the fig tree before Philip called you" (John 1:47-48).

Jesus wanted Nathanael to know that He saw him and that He already knew all about him. Nathanael was shocked and wanted to know how Jesus knew who he was.

Here is what you need to know. In the Bible a fig tree was often the place where people went to be alone with God and to pray or meditate in private. Jesus saw what Nathanael was doing when no one else was watching. Jesus already knew Nathanael's heart.

And guess what? God knows your heart too. So if you ever feel far from God or like no one is paying any attention, you can remember that God always sees you! Keep your eyes open so you can see Him, because just like Nathanael, God wants you to know He is always with you.

Dear God, thank You for seeing and knowing me. Will You help me to love You and to show Your love to others even when it feels like no one is watching? I am happy to know I am not alone! In Jesus's name, amen.

 Remember that God sees you! Write these words on your mirror or on a piece of paper and tape it on a mirror that you look in often: "I See You."

When Will I Be Holy?

Have ever used the word *holy*? Maybe when you were praying to God or talking about Him to someone else? *Holy* is an important word! It is used to describe God's complete perfection and uniqueness. It means He is totally sinless.

The Bible often uses *holy* to describe God, but did you realize that since Jesus's love is in you, He is making you holy too? This simply means God wants your life to be unique and special. He wants your family, friends, and all the people you meet to see your life and the difference He makes.

Hebrews 10:10 says, "We have been made holy through the sacrifice of the body of Jesus Christ once for all." Knowing that you are being made holy probably feels strange or like some impossible job you can never actually complete...and you are right. You cannot become holy on your own. But the Bible says because Jesus died for us, He makes us holy!

When you trust Jesus to forgive your sins, you become one of God's children. He comes into your life and changes you. This is when you begin the process of becoming holy.

Now, this does not mean you are better than anyone else or that you will never make mistakes or bad choices. God calls you holy because His Son, Jesus, lives inside you. But He still has some work to do in you! Being made holy is a daily process. Every day, your job is to grow by being obedient to God.

Becoming holy does not happen overnight, but as you continue to trust God with every part of yourself.

Dear God, I do not always feel holy and special. A lot of the time I feel really plain and ordinary. But I know You are making me more like You each day. Help me to be obedient to You so I can become more like You. Help others to see You in me! In Jesus's name, amen.

 Here are a few more Scriptures to read. Answer the questions based on what you read. This will help you understand more about being holy!

1 Thessalonians 4:7—Who do you need to live holy for?

2 Timothy 1:9—Can you make yourself holy?

1 Peter 1:16—Why do you need to live holy?

Psalm 119:9—How can you keep yourself pure and holy?

What does it mean for you to live a life that is special and set apart—holy?

Why Won't God Change Things Whenever I Ask Him To?

Where I grew up, every few months it would feel different outside. From December through March it was pretty cold and snowy. However, if you did not like the cold, there was nothing to worry about. By April the weather would feel perfect and beautiful flowers would begin to bloom everywhere.

Then right around June the weather would start to change again and it would get really hot outside. This was always fun because that meant school was almost out! Then right around September the weather would begin to get a bit cooler and the leaves on the trees would start turning different shades of red, orange, and golden brown until they finally started to fall off in November.

These changes in the weather are called seasons. As you know, seasons change. If you want to be comfortable and enjoy them, well, then sometimes you have to make a few changes too. For example, the winter would be so cold that every once in a while I would have to wear a snowsuit. Just in case you are wondering, yes, that is the complete opposite of a swimsuit! A snowsuit is a really thick coat with legs. I am pretty sure I looked like an astronaut when I wore it with my snow boots, but it always kept me warm. When it was time for summer, there was no way I would even think about putting on that snowsuit. It was way too hot for that, and I would have been miserable. Not to mention I would have looked pretty strange!

Do the seasons change much where you live? Even if they don't get really cold or really hot, I am sure you need to make certain adjustments every few months so you can go to school or church or the mall comfortably.

Well, guess what? The temperature is not the only thing that changes. Your life has many seasons as well. Have you ever really wanted something to change? Like maybe you can't wait to go to the next grade in school or you really want to be the class president or take a certain dance class? It can be frustrating to want to do something and not be able to do it, but God wants you to know He has designed a time for everything!

God is not just in charge of when the weather changes. He is also in charge of what is happening in your life and when it happens.

Ecclesiastes 3:1 says, "There is a time for everything, and a season for every activity under the heavens."

No matter what may be happening in your life, trust God and ask Him to give you just what you need to be comfortable in the season you are in. Be sure not to rush past a certain season in your life, but ask God to show you the beauty in your season and find out what He wants you to do until He is ready to change things! Just like you can't change the weather, you might not be able to change the season in your life. But God knows just what you need to make it through.

Dear God, I pray that You help me grow in patience! Some seasons can be really fun and some can be hard to handle. Help me trust You and remember that no matter what I am going through, You are in control. In Jesus's name, amen.

Do you keep a journal or a diary? You should! A journal is a great way for you to remember all the seasons in your life. It may seem impossible now, but, I promise, one day you will start to forget some details. Write about your life so you will always remember what God has done for you.

Use this space to start journaling now!

I Know a Lot About God, but What Do I Do with It All?

When I was in sixth grade, I started a new school that was very different from the one I attended before. The uniforms were different and the classes were a lot harder. It was also pretty far from my house. I had to take two buses to get there, all by myself! But one of the biggest differences was that it was a school just for girls. Yes, that means there were no boys in any of my classes. That felt weird at first, but I got used to it pretty quickly.

One of the first things we were going to do as new sixth graders was take an overnight camping trip. We would be gone for four days! I had never been camping and I wasn't really sure if I was going to enjoy it.

My teacher sent home a list of things I would need, and I didn't have any of it at home. So my mom and I took my list and went to a fancy camping store. We bought a sleeping bag, flashlight, rain gear, bug spray, and a bunch of other things. The person working in the store took his time and explained to me what everything was and how to use it. He knew my mother would not be there with me and I needed to learn how to use everything on my own. By the time we left I was well prepared for my first big camping adventure.

I knew what to do if it rained and I knew what to do if it got really hot. I knew what shoes to wear to the lake and I knew how to stay safe at night. I really had everything I needed and my mom made extra sure I was well prepared.

Our parents and people around us can help to prepare us for

the hard things we have to do, but they cannot make us use the things they give us. Going camping with my class and using the supplies my mother bought me was a choice I had to make.

It's just like that with God's Word. Our parents, teachers, and friends help us learn about the Word so we can be prepared for many situations in life. They know there will be some things we have to do on our own, so they try to make sure we are ready.

The Bible says, "Do not forget my teaching, but keep my commands in your heart, for they will prolong your life many years and bring you peace and prosperity" (Proverbs 3:1-2). This verse is God's reminder to us to not only remember the things we learn about Him but to actually use the information to help our lives. How silly would it have been to have all my camping supplies but leave them in the bags?

As you are faced with new and hard situations, remember that if you know and trust God, then you are prepared and have exactly what you need to handle them! Don't leave God's Word packed away. Remember what you hear and learn about Him and choose to use what you know.

Dear God, I know You have given me everything I need. No matter what situation I am in, Your Word will guide me in what I should do. Help me to use what I know about You and my relationship with You to help me grow. In Jesus's name, amen.

 Read Ephesians 6 to find out what special items God has packed away for you to use daily. Write them down to remind yourself of all God has given you!

Why Don't My Friends Listen When I Try to Tell Them the Right Thing to Do?

Has anyone ever asked you to change something? Maybe your mom didn't like your outfit because of the colors or the way it fit. Because she is your mom, you probably listened and changed your outfit, even if you were not happy about it.

Or maybe you are a loud and bubbly person and someone has tried to make you "calm down." Or the opposite—maybe you are really quiet and shy and people try to make you a little more outgoing.

You shouldn't be surprised to know people ask other people to change things all the time. At some point, even you have probably tried to convince someone to do things differently, think differently, or even act differently. I am sure you know that sometimes it works and sometimes it doesn't!

But have you ever tried to change someone's heart? Now, that's a little trickier. Even if you can get someone to change their mind or how they act, it doesn't mean their heart feels any different.

For example, when I was a little girl my neighbor and I used to argue a lot. Our parents always tried to make us get along and not fight, but no matter how hard they tried, it never seemed to last. That is because even after we apologized to each other, our hearts still felt the same as before. We did what we were being asked to do, but we never actually asked God for His help to change us on the inside.

Has anything like this ever happened to you?

Sometimes you may not understand why the people around you are doing the things they are. Watching someone make a bad choice or a choice you disagree with can be frustrating because you think you know what's best for them.

But remember that changing a person's heart is not your job. No person can change another person's heart. Only God can do that! God asks us to be an example of His love. That means sharing His heart with people around us but asking Him to do the rest.

In Ezekiel 36:26-27 God says, "I will give you a new heart and put a new spirit in you; I will remove from you your heart of stone and give you a heart of flesh. And I will put my Spirit in you and move you to follow my decrees and be careful to keep my laws."

This means God is the one who can do it! I know it can be really hard to watch a friend or someone you love make bad choices. But when that happens, never stop showing them and telling them about God's love.

Actually, when you stop trying to change people it becomes easier to love them because you know God does too. The next time you want to tell someone how bad or silly they are for doing what they are doing, decide to pray for them instead. Ask God to place His Spirit in them. God not only wants to change their behavior today; He wants to change their lives forever!

And just remember, He wants to change you too! Don't forget: Before looking for change in someone else, God wants you to look for the things you might need His help with in your own life.

Dear God, help me when I feel tempted to try to change someone. I know You want me to share Your love, and sometimes that means I have to love people even when I really disagree with what they are doing. Help me not to be afraid to speak up when I need to, but to also know You are the only one who can change someone's heart. In Jesus's name, amen.

 Instead of trying to change your friends, choose to pray for them! Here are two Scriptures to read and pray for your friends and for yourself!

James 4:8: Lord, I pray that we would draw close to You.

Romans 12:10: Lord, I pray that I would love them and will look for ways to show Your love.

Is Being Wise the Same as Being Smart?

I like to think I am pretty smart. I can read, write, and figure out most second-grade math problems. Okay, so I am probably not the smartest person you know, but hey, I did get pretty good grades in school.

We have not met, but I just know you are supersmart too!

So let me ask you a question. Have you ever made a not-so-smart choice? You know, like to bite your toenails instead of clipping them or to walk across the kitchen floor in your soccer cleats right after your mom finished mopping it?

Yup. So have I.

You may think your not-so-smart choices do not really matter much. But sometimes they matter a lot. Our choices affect other people and can get us into a lot of trouble.

Like this one time I decided I was going to go to a concert with a friend and her family. The problem is, I asked my mother only about going to my friend's house. I did not tell her about going to the concert. What was I thinking? Of course she found out, and when she did, she was very upset with me. Not telling her about the concert was like lying to her and she could no longer trust me to tell her the truth. Telling a lie is definitely a not-so-smart choice.

The thing is, making bad choices does not have anything to do with how smart you are. It actually has much more to do with how much wisdom you have. Whether you score a 98 or 72 on that really hard math test doesn't matter when it comes to making wise choices.

In Proverbs 2:6 God says, "The LORD gives wisdom; from His mouth come knowledge and understanding." This means that although your teachers and parents can teach you a lot, only God can give you wisdom. He wants to give you a deeper understanding of who He is and what He wants from you. Wisdom is like a secret weapon or code that God only gives His children!

Do you want to know how to get your secret code? Proverbs 9:10 says, "The fear of the LORD is the beginning of wisdom, and knowledge of the Holy One is understanding."

That's right, you have to fear God! Fearing God means to show Him respect (like you would your schoolteacher or a coach) and trust He knows what is best for you.

Sometimes you may be tempted to make your choices based on what you think or how you feel, but do not do that. Seek God for what He says and how He says you need to behave. Ask God to make you wise!

Dear God, thank You for loving me so much that You want me to be wise and make wise choices. I know wisdom comes only from You! Will You help me to understand You more and to know what You want for my life? Help me to be wise, Lord.

Wise or smart? Can you tell the difference? Here are a few things that may seem smart, but are they wise?

Circle "wise" or "not wise" for each statement.

It is wise to always make sure I get what I want.

Wise   Not Wise

It is wise to tell a lie if it keeps me from getting caught.

Wise   Not Wise

It is wise to help others even if it doesn't help me.

Wise   Not Wise

It is wise to share what I have if someone else has a need.

Wise   Not Wise

What Does God Call Me?

Everything has a name.

And by everything, I really mean everything! Think of something, anything, and I bet the first thing you think about it is what you call it. Right?

Names are what give things meaning, and you treat things according to the meaning of their name. For example, when I say *chair*, *tree*, or *shoe*, you know exactly what I am talking about.

So there is no doubt that names are important. And calling something—or some*one*—by their correct name is even more important! If people started calling a school a hospital or a bus a train...well, that would be a little crazy and cause a lot of confusion!

The same is true for people. You have a name; I am sure of it. I am also sure you probably like it when people call you by your correct name or maybe even your nickname.

Do you know what is even more important than the name people call you? It is what God calls you! And here is the thing— God's names for you are actually what give your life its true meaning. What God calls you is actually who you are!

Confused? Let's see if I can help a little.

Your parents have given you a name, and it may even have a really important meaning. However, God gives His children a new name—a new identity, purpose, and meaning. The same way you don't call a chair a shoe or you do not want people to call you a name that is not yours, God does not want you to believe or live like someone He did not create you to be.

God changes who you are.

The Bible says, "If anyone is in Christ, the new creation has come: The old has gone, the new is here!" (2 Corinthians 5:17).

Now, you may not have an actual new name for people to call you, but you definitely have a new meaning to your life once you become God's daughter! Do not let other people call you or say you are something or someone you are not.

Whether your name is Alena, Kaitlyn, Olivia, Camryn, or any other name, God wants you to know you are His child and you are who He says you are!

Dear God, thank You for giving my life meaning. You call me Your daughter and I know that is the best name I could ever have! Help me not to believe anything else people say I am if it disagrees with what You call me. Give me the courage I need to let others know who I am. In Jesus's name, amen.

 People may try to call you all kinds of things that are untrue, but God wants you to know that is not who you are!

Grab a Bible and look at the verses listed below to see what God actually says! Then you have to choose which name you will choose to live like!

I am not afraid.
Deuteronomy 31:6 says I am _____.

I am not ugly.
Song of Solomon 4:7 tells me I am _____.

I am not a failure.
Philippians 4:13 says I can_____.

I am not weak.
Romans 8:37 says I am _____.

I am not mean.
Colossians 3:12 says as God's daughter I am

_____.

I am not unimportant.
John 3:16 says I am so important that God

_____.

I am not guilty.
Psalm 103:12 says I am _____.

What's the Plan?

Do you think about what your life will be like as an adult? Or even as a teenager?

Maybe you have it all planned out and you know exactly where you would like to live, work, and what you will eat for dinner every night. Or maybe you have no idea!

With or without a plan, that feeling of wanting to grow up is normal and it can be fun to imagine the future. But be careful to not try to make it happen too fast. God has a plan for your entire life. That means right now, not just the grown-up part. He has fun and exciting things planned for you, even today!

The Bible says God's plan is good for you, so I encourage you not to miss *any* part of it.

Jeremiah 29:11 says, "'For I know the plans I have for you,' declares the LORD, 'plans to prosper you and not to harm you, plans to give you hope and a future.'"

Yes, sometimes it is hard to know exactly what He is telling you to do, but the more time you spend with Him the better you get to know what He wants for and from your life.

Following the plan God has for you is like playing an exciting game of follow the leader. You just need to go wherever He says to go and do whatever He says to do and you will win. You can trust Him! He is the best leader there is!

Do you ever worry about the future? Ask God to help you to trust Him.

Dear God, thank You for having a plan for my life! I am so excited to see what You have for me when I grow up but I am also excited for today. Help me hear what You are telling me to do and then do it. Teach me to follow You. In Jesus's name, amen.

 Write a letter to yourself! Describe what you want to happen in the next year, what you want to do, what you are expecting, and what changes you want to make. After you write it, put it away for a year. When it is time, open the letter and compare what you wrote to how your year actually went.

Dream big, but always trust that God will surprise you!

Can I Do It?

My brother plays the drums. Even when he was a little boy, he would pick up pencils, sticks, and even straws and bang them on *everything*! He loved playing the drums more than anything else, and he was good at it.

One year for Christmas my mother bought him his very own drum set. I remember exactly what it looked like...and what it sounded like. The drum set was in the basement of our home and every day after school my brother would go down there to practice. Practice meant cymbals, sticks banging, and music blaring!

Can you imagine how loud that sounded?

The cars driving by and the neighbors sitting outside *or inside* their homes could all hear my brother playing his drums. Whenever we had guests over to our home, they would also ask my brother to play something special. We would all gather around and as he ran right to his drums and started playing. He knew being able to play the drums was a gift from God and He was excited and willing to share his gift. People were always so happy to hear him play.

And guess what! As an adult, my brother still plays the drums! It is no longer just a hobby—he actually plays them in church on a stage now! As a little boy, he did not know that God would use his hobby to bless so many other people.

No matter what you enjoy doing, do it to please God. When you focus your attention on pleasing God, it does not matter who is watching or listening!

First Corinthians 10:31 says, "So whether you eat or drink or whatever you do, do it all for the glory of God." Do you have special hobby or talent? Maybe you play an instrument or sport.

Maybe you are a great artist or a storyteller. Whatever talent God has given you, use it for His glory! Do not be shy or try to hide your talents. Be brave and always share your gifts so others can enjoy what God has given you!

Dear God, thank You for giving me gifts and talents. Show me how I can use them to bless other people. Help me to not be shy or embarrassed but to be confident because You have given them to me. In Jesus's name, amen.

Use this space to brainstorm how you can use your talents! Remember that whatever your gift is, God can use it to bless someone else. For example, you could use your talents to make crafts as gifts for friends, write a song for your baby sister, or color or draw a picture for your teacher. You have so many options!

What Are the Gifts of Grace and Mercy?

Can you think of a time someone gave you a gift? Maybe they gave you a birthday gift or a present for getting good grades or doing all your chores. But can you think of a time when someone gave you a gift in place of a punishment?

It would be awfully strange if you disobeyed your mom or dad, but when they came into your room to punish you, instead they handed you a beautifully wrapped package with a huge bow on top!

Or what if someone told you that every time you did something wrong they would take your punishment? You would probably think they were playing some strange trick on you, right?

But that is exactly what God did by sending Jesus to die for us! The Bible tells us our sin should lead to punishment. But God showed us grace and mercy by sending His Son instead of giving us what we deserve. Jesus took all our punishment so we could have life now and forever. This is salvation! God loves us that much!

Grace is getting what you don't deserve, like a present you did not earn. If you trust Jesus to forgive you of your sins, then you have received God's gift of grace. Mercy is not getting what you deserve. Even though the wrong things you do deserve punishment, Jesus already took that punishment for you.

Doesn't this make you really happy?

The Bible says in Romans 6:23, "The wages of sin is death, but the gift of God is eternal life in Christ Jesus our Lord."

Sin deserves a punishment, but instead God gave us life! John 3:16 says, "For God so loved the world that he gave his one and only Son, that whoever believes in him shall not perish but have eternal life."

Thank God for His grace and mercy!

Dear God, thank You for giving me life now and forever with You. Please help me grow in my understanding of how much You love me. In Jesus's name, amen.

 One of the best ways to thank God for His grace and mercy is by giving grace and mercy to someone else! The next time someone does something wrong to you, choose to be gracious with your words and with your actions. In other words, choose to be kind even when you think someone doesn't deserve it.

What If I Do Not Want What I Have?

Pretend someone walked up to you and your friends and handed each of you a ball. Then they looked at you and said, "I have a game I want you to play." Before they told you what the game was, you noticed that each of your friends had a different kind of ball. Some were big and some were small. The balls were different colors and shapes. Your ball was orange and looked like a basketball. Some of the others looked like soccer balls, footballs, and volleyballs.

After seeing all the balls, you decided you did not want the ball you received because some of the others looked better. You just knew they would have more fun with their balls than you would with yours. So you started crying and begged for a different ball until someone agreed to switch with you. Someone traded a smaller, hard white ball for your orange ball.

You were very happy with your new ball and it was just what you wanted—until you found out the game you were going to play was basketball!

Now you had a problem. It would be really hard to play a game of basketball using a baseball, wouldn't it?

Instead of trusting that you had the ball you needed, you wanted what was given to someone else. Now you couldn't even enjoy the game.

Have you ever wanted what someone else has? Maybe an outfit your sister had, a toy your friend had, or even something bigger, like the house your neighbor lived in. Wanting what someone else has is called *coveting*. The Bible says you should not covet because God has given you just want you need. Do not try to have what others have. The life God wants for you is different from what He wants for someone else. Instead of trying to get what others have, focus on what God has given you for the game He has planned for you to play.

Get it? Maybe the Bible can help. Hebrews 13:5 says, "Keep your lives free from the love of money and be content with what you have." What are you grateful for today?

Dear God, thank You for everything You have given me. Help me to be grateful and confident that You have given me everything I need to do what You need me to do. In Jesus's name, amen.

What are you grateful for today? Write a letter thanking God for the things He has given you.

Am I a Disciple?

I want to introduce you to 12 very special men in the Bible. Their names are Simon (also called Peter), Andrew, James, John, Philip, Bartholomew, Matthew, Thomas, James, Simon, Judas the son of James, and Judas Iscariot.

Have you heard these names before? You can read all about their lives in the New Testament. These 12 men were Jesus's closest followers—His disciples. They followed Jesus and told everyone about Him. A disciple is a student or a follower who learns everything they can from their leader.

Jesus's disciples wanted everyone to know He was the Son of God and had come to save them. People did not always believe them, but they continued to share with as many people as they could about Jesus's life anyway.

The 12 disciples prayed with people, helped them in different ways, and did whatever Jesus asked them to do. They were examples of God's love by being as much like Jesus as they could.

But they did not always get it right! They made mistakes. Sometimes they were afraid, and one of them, Peter, even pretended not to know Jesus when he was afraid he would be hurt or killed.

Being Jesus's followers did not make them perfect, but Jesus loved them and wanted them to be close to Him. He wanted them to see how He lived so they could show others. He wanted them to know He forgave them when they made mistakes because He wanted them to know how to forgive others. Jesus wanted them to know and learn everything about Him so they could teach others everything they learned.

This is what Jesus wanted from His disciples, and this is what

He wants from you! In John 8:31 Jesus says, "If you hold to my teaching, you are really my disciples."

Are you learning about Jesus and asking Him to help you be like Him? Are you teaching others what you know? Being Jesus's disciple starts with trusting Him as your teacher and leader. Once you are following Him, encourage and ask others to follow Jesus with you.

Dear God, help me follow You and encourage others to follow You too. Thank You for helping me learn from You and do what You do. In Jesus's name, amen.

 Read Matthew 28:16-19. What two things does Jesus tell His disciples to do?

1.

2.

Can you do these things too?

Do I Have to Forgive Them?

Have you ever ignored someone or treated a friend badly because you just could not forgive them for something they did? Maybe you stopped talking to them or yelled at them, or even tried to hurt them. How did that make you feel?

I am sure it did not feel good to be hurt, but have you ever noticed that being mean or trying to get back at someone does not feel good either? Plus, it can be a lot of work!

I have good news for you: Forgiving people may not be easy, but it will always be better in the end. You can and you should forgive people who hurt you. The Bible says no matter what they have done to you and even if they do not ask you to forgive them first, forgiving them is best. "Bear with each other and forgive one another if any of you has a grievance against someone. Forgive as the Lord forgave you" (Colossians 3:13).

You might still be sad or even angry for what they did, but God says you should forgive anyway. God did not just forgive you one time; He keeps forgiving you over and over again! And He wants you to do the same with other people. Forgiveness helps you feel better because you don't keep thinking about how much someone has hurt you. Instead you focus on God's love. Forgiveness also makes the person you are forgiving feel better. You see, when you choose to forgive, you are being an example of God's love to someone else.

Forgiving is not always easy, but you cannot just wait until you feel like it. Sometimes you have to just do it. So is there someone who needs to know you forgive them? Maybe they have asked for your forgiveness but you still treat them differently. Choose to forgive. It is a choice you can make!

Dear God, it really hurts my feelings when someone is mean to me. I know I need to forgive them just like You forgive me, but it is hard. Will You help me treat them kindly even though I do not like what they did? Give me the courage to let them know I forgive them. In Jesus's name, amen.

 Read Matthew 18:21-35 and rewrite this story in your own words. What do you think the servant should have done differently? What would you have done?

Have I Ever Hurt Jesus?

Do you have a best friend? Do you ever fight or argue? When I was in third grade my best friend and I started to fight a lot. We had been best friends since kindergarten and then suddenly she just started to treat me pretty mean. She would tease me in front of other people and she stopped wanting to play with me. I could not figure out why, but she just did not seem to like me anymore. I felt so sad and betrayed. Someone I trusted had hurt me.

Has anything like this ever happened to you? Someone you used to be friends with started to treat you mean or talk about you in a bad way to other people? Betrayal does not feel good, but you are not alone. The Bible says even Jesus was betrayed by someone He was close to—Judas.

Judas was one of Jesus's disciples, the 12 men who were closest to Jesus while He was here on earth. However, Judas was the one to turn Jesus in to the Pharisees. The Pharisees were the people who wanted to kill Him. Judas knew what would happen to Jesus when the Pharisees found Him, and he betrayed Him anyway.

You may be wondering how Judas could do that to Jesus! As one of the disciples, Judas had seen how much Jesus loved everyone and all the great things He did for people. What do you think you would have done? Do you think you would have ever betrayed Him?

It's sad, but God's people still betray Jesus sometimes, even today. Think about it like this: Have you ever listened to people say mean or untrue things about Him and decided not to take a stand? Maybe it felt better to be liked or to do what the other people were doing. Betrayal does not feel good when someone does it to you, and it does not feel good if you do it to God.

Just like Judas, you have seen how good Jesus is. Don't ever decide to stop choosing to be on His side. No one can offer you anything better than Jesus can!

Dear God, I know what You have for me is better than anything anyone else can give me. Thank You for forgiving me when I don't stand up for You. Thank You for Your love for me. In Jesus's name, amen.

Here are three ways you can choose God!

1. Never be too shy or afraid to tell others about God's love and what He means to you.
2. Talk to Him often in prayer.
3. Spend time learning more about God and the difference He makes in your life.

What If I Am Not Tired?

Are you awake? Well, of course you are. But are you wide awake and alert? Or are you a little tired and groggy?

I know you may not like it when it's time to go to bed at night, but sleep really is good for you. It's important that you get the rest you need to feel strong and healthy. When you are awake but tired, you do not feel your best and it is hard to be your best. You may be grumpy and you can miss important things that are happening around you. And you may fall asleep when you are supposed to be awake—like while you are watching a movie with friends or during school! Have you ever been in a class at school or church when the teacher had to call someone's name to get them to wake up? It can be pretty embarrassing!

It actually even happened in the Bible to a young man named Eutychus. Eutychus was about your age and he had been listening to Paul talk about God for a while. He fell asleep while listening and tumbled out of a window! Can you believe that? Acts 20:9-10 tells us,

> Seated in a window was a young man named Eutychus, who was sinking into a deep sleep as Paul talked on and on. When he was sound asleep, he fell to the ground from the third story and was picked up dead. Paul went down, threw himself on the young man and put his arms around him. "Don't be alarmed," he said. "He's alive!"

You might not sleep where you can fall out of a window, but God wants you to be awake when you are supposed to be. He wants you to be alert and able to enjoy all the things happening in your day! This means you have to be willing to rest when it is time to rest. Don't get upset when it is time to sleep. Instead, thank God for helping you to rest so you can enjoy your day.

Dear God, thank You for helping me to know when I need to rest. I want to be awake and alert so I can hear and see everything You have for me! In Jesus's name, amen.

 Sometimes you may not want to admit when you are sleepy, but there is nothing wrong with needing rest. Your body will let you know it's time to sleep. For example, do you yawn or become cranky or sad when you're tired? Make a list of the ways your body lets you know it's sleepy. When you notice these things happening, then you know it's time for you to rest!

What Is the Difference Between Prideful and Humble?

Have you ever felt really special because of something you have done? Maybe you have been an amazing friend or a fantastic daughter. Maybe you are the star on your soccer team or you are always the first one to know the answer in class. Maybe everyone keeps telling you how awesome you are. It feels good when that happens, doesn't it?

This is when you have to be careful. When you start to feel too important because of your achievements, pray and ask God to help you to stay humble.

Being humble is the opposite of being prideful, and here is the difference: A prideful person brags about who they are or what they do, and they love to be noticed by others. But a humble person does not take credit for the good things that happen. They know God is the reason for everything they are able to do.

The Bible says being humble is a much better choice! "When pride comes, then comes disgrace, but with humility comes wisdom" (Proverbs 11:2). There is nothing wrong with knowing you are special, but always remember why you are special—you are God's precious daughter! And it is His kindness that brings every good thing into your life.

When you are humble, you can relax and trust God because you know you are only able to do what you do because of His help.

Pray and ask God to help you to not be prideful but to be humble and grateful for Him.

Dear God, thank You for all You let me do. Help me always remember that I am important because I am Your creation. You are the only reason I am who I am. I pray that You will teach me more about humility and help me to stay humble. In Jesus's name, amen.

 Being humble takes practice, but all you have to do is do it! When you accomplish or achieve something great, thank God before you do anything else as a way to remind yourself that He is the only reason you can do anything.

Do My Friends Know I Love Them?

When someone gives you a gift, how do you act? Do you jump up and down, throw your arms around the person, and scream, "Thank you!" while spinning in circles?

Or maybe you are more of a quiet person, so you just smile and say a soft and sweet, "Thank you."

However you choose to say thank you (soft or loud, standing still or running in circles), I am sure that on the inside you are super excited about your gift!

Gifts are special, and when someone gives you one, it is really important to make sure you show them how grateful you are by saying thank you with your mouth and with your heart. A part of saying thank you with your heart means you take care of the gift.

How rude would it be if someone gave you a gift but then they saw it in the trash can or tossed on the floor in a corner under your dirty clothes or inside a leftover pizza box the next time they visited you? That would be so rude, right? What would they think and how would they feel?

Well, good friends are one of the best gifts you will ever get! Having someone to laugh with, talk to, and spend time with is very special.

If you have a friend you enjoy spending time with, make sure she knows it! Show her with your heart! Treat her well and love her always, just like you would a special gift. Don't just toss your friendships in a corner with the trash. Instead of getting into fights over silly things, love your friends at all times—just like the Bible tells us to. Just like any good gift, a friendship is too important for you to just throw away or treat badly.

How can you let your friends know how special they are today?

....

Dear God, help me be a good friend and love my friends at all times. Remind me of how good a friend You are to me so I can remember to be the same to others. In Jesus's name, amen.

 Taking the time to make something for friends is a great way to let them know how much you love them. Make a few of these Friendship Flowers and give them to a special friend! You will need:

- Construction paper
- Scissors
- Glue

1. Cut the construction paper into two-inch-wide strips, length of your choice. Make a thin fold along any one of the edges of the strips.

2. Cut the paper strip horizontally, but not all the way through. Leave a half inch of the strip along the folded vertical edges intact. Try to cut all the fringes equally and also try to keep the fringes as thin as possible. The thinner the fringes the prettier the flower!

3. Make swirly patterns by rolling each strip one by one in the same direction. Start rolling each strip from its end and all the way through the other end. Take your time and make the swirls carefully. This will help your flower to have a beautiful pattern!

4. Use green paper to make the stem for your flower. Cut a long strip of green craft paper and start rolling the paper diagonally from any one corner, and keep rolling the paper till you reach the other end. Secure the paper on both ends by applying a small amount of glue.

5. Now apply glue along the intact part of the swirly-fringed paper. Wrap the glued part of the swirly-fringed paper onto the green rolled paper. Start from the top of the stem and carefully roll it toward the bottom of the stem. Keep rolling (and gluing) until the swirly paper ends.

How Am I Supposed to Love Someone Who Is Mean to Me?

Are you God's girl? What do you think that means? For starters, it means you are kind and thoughtful and that you love others. It means you look for ways to help others, that you forgive people, and that you do your best to show God's love always. Mostly it means you seek God's grace and purpose for your life with all you have.

Being God's girl also means you make wise choices even when it is hard. This means you use the information you have to help you make good decisions. Sometimes you have to choose to protect yourself from something that hurts you. This can be confusing because you know God wants you to be kind and to love everyone—which is true even when people do not love you back! However, that doesn't mean you should let others hurt you or treat you badly. Being God's girl means you ask Him to help you handle every situation you face.

First Peter 5:8 gives us a warning. "Be alert and of sober mind. Your enemy the devil prowls around like a roaring lion looking for someone to devour." God wants you to pay attention and be careful because the devil is always looking for ways to hurt you, and he will use anything he can to do it. For example, if you have a classmate who always teases you and says mean things about you to others, you probably need to keep your distance from her.

Always remember that making choices to protect yourself does not mean it's okay to treat people badly or say rude things. Instead it means you love them anyway and pray for them. Ask

God to touch their hearts so they will know His love and will want to love God and others too!

Dear God, help me to be wise and know how to protect myself from hurtful people and things. Mostly, help me to love those who want to hurt me and show them Your love. In Jesus's name, amen.

 The best way to show love to someone is to pray for him or her! If you have someone you need to protect your heart from, say this prayer for them.

Dear God,

I know You see the problems I am having with

_____.

I know You love them and I pray that You will show them Your love. I know I need to love them too.

Will You fill _____'s heart with joy?

Help _____ with anything hard that [she/he] is dealing with and help me to be patient and kind to [her/him].

Am I a Leader?

When you are with your friends, do you enjoy being in charge and making up the rules to a new game? Do you like giving everyone instructions for how to play? Or would you rather see what others are doing and help them with what they need?

I bet you enjoy a little bit of both—leading others in some ways and helping out in others! Whichever you enjoy the most, do not feel bad about it! Leading and following are very important and both are needed.

Every team needs a coach and every coach needs a team, right? Could there even be a soccer team without a coach? Or what good is a coach without the team? It just would not work! They need each other to play.

Being able to lead others is a gift and being able to work well with other people is a gift too. In Matthew 20:26 Jesus says, "Whoever wants to become great among you must be your servant." Think about Jesus, the Son of God. Jesus is always our example and the Bible says He is both a leader and a servant. As God's Son, He is in charge but He leads by helping others.

The next time you are trying to get your friends or little brother or sister to do something, do not just boss them around! Be patient. Show them how to do it and think of how you can help them.

Dear God, help me to lead. Help me to follow. Thank You for teaching me that serving others is how I start being a leader. In Jesus's name, amen.

 Read John 13:1-17. In your own words, describe what Jesus is doing in this passage. Why do you think He does this? What example is Jesus setting for you? How can you lead by serving today?

What If God Is Not Real?

Have you ever asked yourself, "What if God is not real?"

You don't have to be embarrassed about asking that question. God can handle it. He wants you to know and believe how real He is!

Now, if you have never struggled to believe that God is real, that's great!

The Bible actually says you are blessed when you believe Him even though you have never seen Him (read John 20:29).

However, if you have had problems believing, I just want you to know you are not alone.

Many people have tried to prove God's existence by studying history and science. But the Bible tells us believing God requires faith. That means you have to believe Him and that He is real even though you cannot physically see Him with your eyes.

Thomas was one of Jesus's disciples, which means he had the privilege of following Jesus on earth and seeing Him with his own eyes. Thomas talked to Jesus, listened to Him, and saw the many miracles He performed. As you can imagine, Thomas had no problems believing Jesus while He was with Him. However, after Jesus was hung on the cross, Thomas struggled to believe He had risen from the grave. He had seen with his own eyes how badly Jesus was beaten, then had died and was buried. So when the other disciples tried to tell him Jesus was alive again, Thomas did not believe them.

He just had to see Jesus for himself. So do you know what Jesus did? Read this!

Thomas...one of the Twelve, was not with the disciples when Jesus came. So the other disciples told him, "We have seen the Lord!"

But he said to them, "Unless I see the nail marks in his hands and put my finger where the nails were, and put my hand into his side, I will not believe."

A week later his disciples were in the house again, and Thomas was with them. Though the doors were locked, Jesus came and stood among them and said, "Peace be with you!" (John 20:24-26).

Jesus visited the disciples, and because He knew about Thomas and his disbelief, He told Thomas to reach out his hand and touch the scars from where He had been beaten and hung on the cross.

Jesus cared about Thomas and wanted him to believe. He told him, "Put your finger here; see my hands. Reach out your hand and put it into my side. Stop doubting and believe" (John 20:27).

So maybe you can feel just how Thomas felt and you need to see for yourself.

Well, I have good news for you! You can ask Jesus to show Himself to you. Unlike Thomas, you will not be able to touch His physical body. However, you can see Jesus in many other ways and in many other places. Look around at the sunset, the ocean, your best friend's smile. You are surrounded by God's presence!

Pray and ask God to increase your faith and to help you to see His presence every day.

Dear God, I want to believe in You but sometimes I have doubt. I know I need to have faith. Will You help me to always believe that You are real and what You say is true? Will You help me to see You in my life and help my faith to grow even when I can't see You around me? Take away my doubts so I can believe and live for You! In Jesus's name, amen.

Finish these sentences!

I have a hard time believing God is real when

_____.

I know God is real because

_____.

I feel God's presence most when

_____.

What Am I Thinking?

When I was a little girl, we went to church often. We went on Sunday mornings and came back for a second service on Sunday afternoons. We also went to Bible Study on Wednesday evenings, and there were services on Fridays as well. We did not go to every service, but we definitely went to a lot of them!

Mostly, I enjoyed going to church because my friends were there. There was usually a program for the children to attend while the adults were in their service, and we always did something fun.

But every once in a while I would have to go to "big" service with my mom and grandmother. And that was when things got a little complicated. It was always hard to sit through the service and pay attention. It seemed that no matter how hard I tried my mind just would not let me focus. I would start thinking about school, camp, roller coasters...and that really funny story my brother told me at dinner! All types of thoughts would take over my mind, and it felt like I could not control it.

Have you ever felt like that? Maybe not in church, but perhaps all you can think about while sitting in English class is lunch. Or when you are on your way to sleep, your mind begins to think about scary things. Or you can't stop thinking about how angry you are with that boy who tripped you in the gym. Or maybe you are thinking too much about the next exciting thing you are going to do.

You may not realize it, but your thoughts matter a lot, and controlling your mind can be difficult. Not all thoughts are good for you! For example, mean or scary thoughts will affect your behavior and the choices you make.

God wants your mind to be full of Him and for your thoughts

to point to Him and His love. In the Bible He tells us, "Set your minds on things above, not on earthly things" (Colossians 3:2).

God knows if we spend too much time thinking only about the things we can see and how we feel, then we will miss focusing on Him!

God's Word can change everything. For example, do you have problems paying attention in one of your classes? Proverbs 4:25 says, "Let your eyes look straight ahead; fix your gaze directly before you." This is just a simple reminder that if you look straight ahead, then you have a better chance of not missing something important!

Want to know how you can set your mind on what is before you? Here are five tips to help you.

1. Read your Bible often. This helps to fill your mind with thoughts of Jesus and gives you an example for how to live your life. You can also find special Scriptures and post them around. Some good places to put a verse or two are in your closet, on your notebook, or on your mirror.

2. Listen to worship music. Sometimes our thoughts can really get out of control, especially when we are afraid or angry. When this happens, find a few worship songs you love and play them over and over again. Singing songs to and about God is a great way to help control the other things you may be thinking about.

3. Be careful what you watch. Watching your favorite TV shows is not a bad thing. However, sometimes the shows we watch can affect how we think about our parents, our friends, and our lives. Be sure to choose shows that make you love God and people around you more. If a show is giving you thoughts that make you talk to your sister, mom, or dad in a way that doesn't please God, ask yourself, "Should I be watching this?"

4. Spend time with people who love God. Just like the shows we watch, the people we spend time with can influence our thoughts. If your friends gossip a lot, treat each other unkindly, or make bad choices, that behavior will definitely rub off on you and your thoughts! Try to spend time with people who are "like-minded" and want to keep their eyes on God too.

5. Ask God to help. Pray and ask God to help you to keep your thoughts on Him and His love. God is always waiting to help us and loves when we ask Him for what we need.

Dear God, thank You for giving me a brain that can think! Sometimes it gets hard to keep my mind focused on You because there are so many distractions around me. Will You help me to remember that the more I look to You, the more I will understand and know what You want me to do? In Jesus's name, amen.

Philippians 4:8 reminds us, "Whatever is true, whatever is noble, whatever is right, whatever is pure, whatever is lovely, whatever is admirable—if anything is excellent or praiseworthy—think about such things."

Can you rewrite that Scripture verse in your own words? What do you think God is saying to you? Don't be afraid to use a dictionary or ask for help if you are not sure what some of the words mean!

Do I Have to Be Brave?

have one brother and he is five years older than me. Having an older brother is really cool. As a little girl, it meant I always had a great friend to play with and a fun babysitter! It was just the two of us and we were really close. I loved being his little sister and I looked up to him so much.

I have many memories and fun stories of things my brother and I did. Like building cars from the couch cushions and making a special racetrack for our pet hermit crabs!

One night my mother went out and, as usual, my brother had a list of things we were going to do to have fun. Somehow our list wasn't long enough, and after listening to music, playing video games, and watching our favorite TV shows, we were bored. My brother decided we should do something adventurous, so we went upstairs to my mother's bedroom, opened the window, and climbed out. Yes, that's right. We climbed out onto the roof of our front porch!

Please do not ever do this!

We both knew this was a bad idea, but because I looked up to my brother so much, I decided not to say anything and to go along with his plan.

Yes—that was another bad idea. I did not want to be the one to ruin the fun.

Thankfully, our neighbor saw us on the roof before we got hurt and he made us go back into the house. Of course, he also told my mother when she got home, and she was not happy about our bad decision at all!

When she asked me why I did it, all I could say was, "Because my brother did it!" As you can imagine, that was not a good enough answer and we both got into really big trouble!

I know my brother did not mean to get me into trouble, and it wasn't his fault entirely. I should have been brave enough to tell him I thought it was a bad idea, but I wasn't.

Has something like this ever happened to you? If you have brothers and sisters then I am sure it has! No, you probably have not gone onto your roof (and remember, *never* do that!), but you have probably done something with them you knew you shouldn't do. You may have been more interested in having fun or, maybe, like me, you just didn't want to be the one to ruin the fun.

Sometimes it can be hard to say no to your closest friends. But going along with a bad choice is really dangerous. You may get hurt, hurt someone else, or just do something that is not good for your life. With your siblings and with your friends you can decide to be the one who is not afraid to do the right thing.

God wants you to be bold and brave. Being bold does not mean you are mean or bossy. Being bold means when you are faced with a choice, you are not afraid to speak up in love and do the right thing.

Ask God to give you courage! And when you need to be bold, remember Psalm 138:3: "When I called, you answered me; you greatly emboldened me."

Dear God, sometimes it's easy for me to speak up for You, but sometimes it can be really hard. Will You teach me the importance of being bold? Give me the strength I need to be brave. Teach me to always speak to others with love. In Jesus's name, amen.

Need a little encouragement? Well, the Bible tells the stories of plenty of girls and women just like you who made really brave decisions for God. They spoke up with their words and their actions and are great examples for you. Read their stories. When you are brave for God, you are not alone!

For Rahab's story, read Joshua 2.

For Esther's story, read Esther 1–10.

For Lydia's story, read Acts 16.

Who Is God?

What is your name?

Do you like it?

Does it have a special meaning or story behind why your family chose that name for you? Maybe it was your great-grandmother's name, or maybe your family just thought it sounded really pretty.

The writers of the Bible used many different names to describe God. These different names help us understand His character. God doesn't want you to have to guess what He acts like or who He really is. He wants you to know Him and to trust His actions!

So let's pretend I'm introducing you to God for the very first time. I know, you probably already know Him, but let's see what His name teaches us about how He acts and who He wants to be in our lives.

Let's have fun with this! Here we go:

I'd like you to meet...

Jehovah: The "I Am who I Am."

Jehovah tells you God is a person. This is a characteristic you want to remember because it lets you know we serve a very real and very personal God! He wants to be in relationship with you.

Second, I'd like to introduce you to...

Jehovah Jireh: "The Lord our Provider."

Jireh means God wants to give you everything you need. This should put your heart at ease because it reminds you that God knows exactly what you need, even when you don't, and that He has all the power and ability to bring those things into your life.

Third, meet...

Jehovah Tsaba: "The Lord our Warrior."

Don't be afraid! God is with you in any battle you face. He is protecting you and He is fighting for you! Is there something that you don't want to face alone? Don't worry. God is the best soldier who could ever come to your rescue!

Fourth, here is...

Jehovah Shalom: "The Lord is Peace."

Do you ever feel anxious, afraid, overwhelmed? When you do, remember that God *is* your peace. Keep your mind focused on Him and spend time with Him and you can stay calm, even in the scariest moments.

Last, allow me to introduce to you to...

Jehovah Rohi: "The Lord my Shepherd."

Yes, you and I are like sheep. We get hungry, scared, and lost, and we sometimes put ourselves in danger. But God is our shepherd. You can rest knowing He is in complete control. You can always depend on Him!

These are just a few of the names God uses to teach us about His character. The more you understand who God really is, the more you love Him and trust Him to take care of you!

Dear God, thank You for being You and for loving me! Will You help me to get to know and understand all of Your characteristics? I am excited to know more about You! In Jesus's name, amen.

Which of God's names that you just learned means the most to you? Why?

Does God Love Me as Much as He Loved People in the Bible?

I've got a few great stories to tell you.

Moses and thousands of Israelites were trying to leave Egypt, where they had been slaves and were treated very unkindly. God sent Moses to lead them from Egypt, but when they came to the Red Sea (a really big body of water!) they thought they were stuck because they did not know how they would get to the other side. The Egyptians were coming to attack them, and there was a huge sea in front of them!

You have to read Exodus 14 for all the details, but what you need to know is that God split the sea and made a path for the Israelites to walk across!

Whoa! God must have loved them a lot, huh?

Maybe you already know the story of Lazarus. Lazarus was the brother of Mary and Martha. He was Jesus's friend. Lazarus died and everyone was very sad—including Jesus. But Jesus had another plan! Jesus called Lazarus from his grave and brought him back to life. Don't believe me? Read it for yourself in Luke 11.

These stories and many more from the Bible show all the amazing things God will do for the people who accept His love for them.

And I've got great news! The God who parted the Red Sea and raised Lazarus from the dead is the same God who is listening to you and hears your prayers. Yes, sometimes it may feel like God is only interested in what is happening in other people's lives, but do not believe that. He loves and cares for you just as much as He loved and cared for Moses, the Israelites, and Lazarus.

God is interested in the details. He cares about the small things as well as the big things in your life. Talk to Him about it all and watch the special ways He shows His love for you.

Dear God, thank You for using the stories of people like Moses and Lazarus to remind me of how much You love Your children, including me! Thank You for loving me! Help me to know that You will do amazing things in my life too.

 Make a scrapbook of all the amazing things God has done in your life! Remember, there is nothing too small or too big, because He cares about it all! A scrapbook is a great way to remember all He has done.

Here is what you need to make a scrapbook:

- Card stock
- Scissors
- Glue stick
- Markers
- 2 or 3 of your favorite pictures (but because you may have to cut them, ask an adult first!). If you do not have pictures, draw some!
- Embellishments (Be creative! You can use anything, like stickers, old earrings, or buttons.)

Here is what you need to do:

1. Gather your supplies.

2. Using your card stock, photos, and embellishments, lay out your page. Try different designs until you get everything the way you like it.

3. Glue the pieces in place on your card stock.

4. Journal: Write down what you want to remember about the picture and why what God did is amazing. Include the date, where you were, names of people you were with, and what you were doing.

5. Repeat steps 1 through 4 and create several pages.

Be sure to write down anything else that makes that picture special. And be creative! Use as many colors and designs as you want.

Are Any Other Girls like Me?

Have you ever thought about this: There are millions of Christians all over the world! Seriously, millions! This means a lot of people love Jesus and God's love is everywhere.

This also means many families like yours and girls just like you love Jesus and want to follow Him. They speak many different languages. Their churches probably look different from yours. They may even wear a different style of clothes when they go to church.

But do you know what? None of that even matters! If you love Jesus then you have something in common with other girls all over the world!

Some people even live in places where they are treated unkindly because of their love for Jesus. It may be hard for you to think about living in a place where loving Jesus is dangerous, but unfortunately, many people are forced to live like this. They have to hide their Bibles and protect their churches and families.

Can you believe that anyone would not want you to love Jesus?

But God's love is bigger than any danger!

No matter where you live, or what your church looks like, God loves all His children the same.

That is good news, right?

John 3:16 says, "God so loved the world that he gave his one and only Son, that whoever believes in him shall not perish but have eternal life." That is pretty awesome. It means girls all over the world are loved by God and can have Him in their lives now and forever.

So here is what I want you to do. Choose a place in the world (Germany, Australia, Canada, America, Uganda, China, the Bahamas...ask an adult to help you choose a place if you can't decide) and pray for the Christians there. Especially the Christian girls who are just like you!

Can you do that? Can you pray that God keeps them safe and helps them to learn more about Him? You can also pray that they are bold and brave and will tell others about God's love! You can ask God for that same bravery as well.

Dear God, thank You for the way You love everyone. Will You help me care about Your children around the world? Teach me to pray for them and to support them. Thank You for making me Yours!

 Take a few minutes and write your prayer for the people in your chosen country here. Repeat this prayer as often as you want, asking God to bless other Christians around the world and help others see His love through girls just like you.

How Can I Do Everything God Asks Me to Do?

Do you like grapes? I think they're so yummy—especially when they're big and juicy. I just love the really dark purple ones. They are perfect for a good bite-sized snack!

Grapes are a fruit. I bet you already knew that, right? When someone asks if you like grapes, you probably only think of two types—purple grapes and green grapes.

Do you know there are thousands of different types of grapes? Grapes can actually be up to seven different colors, including black, red, and a golden color, and each type has a different taste. Also, grapes are fairly easy to grow. They can survive in different environments, which means they can grow in many places around the world.

Did you know grapes were around when Jesus was on earth? He even used them to explain our relationship with Him.

In John 15:5 Jesus says, "I am the vine; you are the branches. If you remain in me and I in you, you will bear much fruit; apart from me you can do nothing."

God is not calling us grapes or branches here, but He is using grapes and how they grow to teach us something important. If you read your Bible, then you may have noticed that He does this type of thing often—and not just with grapes!

So to understand this verse, here is what you need to know: Grapes are fruit that are produced on a grapevine. They grow in clusters directly on a branch attached to a healthy and strong grapevine.

So when you read John 15:15, think about it this way: God

compares us to the branches because of our need to stay connected to Him, the vine. If we want our lives to produce good fruit, like grapes, then we (the branches) need to stay connected to God (the vine).

Now do you get it?

God created us to need Him. It would be a little weird to see a cluster of delicious and juicy grapes growing on a branch, sitting on the ground, disconnected from the vine. Without the vine to give it the nourishment and support it needs, it would be impossible for a branch to remain healthy and produce a cluster of delicious grapes. In fact, it would die pretty fast, right?

So the next time you are feeling overwhelmed, sad, afraid, or unproductive, check to make sure you are still connected to the Vine, Jesus, your source of support and nourishment!

Often we know what God expects us to do, like being kind and making wise choices, but we think we have to do it on our own. God wants you to know that you do not. In fact, He knows you cannot produce anything good without being close and connected to Him.

Dear God, thank You for being my support and strength. I pray that my life produces good fruit. Help me to stay connected to You and remind me to seek You when I feel discouraged or far away, because You always know just what I need. In Jesus's name, amen.

Think of a time when you feel overwhelmed. Now that you know God is your source, how can you ask Him to help you in this situation?

Who Is the Holy Spirit?

Have you ever seen a crossing guard? If you go to school or have driven by a school in the early morning or mid-afternoon, then you probably have. The guards are usually adults wearing bright orange or yellow vests. They carry huge red signs in the shape of an octagon with the word *STOP* on them and they stay very close to the corner of busy streets.

Crossing guards have an important job. They help pedestrians, mostly schoolchildren, cross the street safely. *Pedestrian* is just a big word for people who are walking. So a crossing guard's main job is to protect children from traffic and danger while they are on an important journey.

Being a crossing guard is a huge responsibility. Their job is to prevent danger.

Has a crossing guard ever helped you before?

You can trust crossing guards because they are well prepared and know just what to do to keep everyone safe. As soon as they see children or people coming, they walk out into the street holding their STOP sign up high to stop the cars and clear the path for everyone to cross safely.

Drivers know to stop and pedestrians know to walk quickly when they see this happening. However, it would be really difficult for crossing guards to do their job if the pedestrians or drivers decided not to obey them! That would cause so much chaos and someone would probably get hurt.

When it comes to our relationship with God, I think you and I are a lot like pedestrians. We are on an important journey and we need someone to help guide us, hold up a STOP sign, and clear the path to keep us out of danger.

I have good news! God has given each of His children their very own crossing guard. John 16:13 says, "When he, the Spirit of truth, comes, he will guide you into all the truth. He will not speak on his own; he will speak only what he hears, and he will tell you what is yet to come."

Before Jesus returned to heaven, He promised to send a helper to His people, and He did! This helper is the Holy Spirit.

The Holy Spirit is a person of the Trinity. It can be a little confusing to understand, but know that God the Father, God the Son, and God the Holy Spirit—together known as the Trinity—are all the same God, and you can trust that He knows just what to do.

God sees what is coming our way and He has sent His Holy Spirit to guide us through difficult situations safely.

Are you willing to listen to the Holy Spirit when He is telling you not to go in a certain direction or to stop doing something you are doing? Are you willing to follow His guidance down a different path?

You may not be able to hear the Holy Spirit's instructions, but when you know God's Word (by reading your Bible) and spend time talking to God, then you can trust that the Holy Spirit will speak to your heart and guide you in the right direction.

Dear God, thank You for sending me a guide. I am so grateful that You want to keep me safe and that You do not leave me alone when dangerous situations are coming my way. Will You help me to be obedient and to follow Your instructions?

Want to know about the Holy Spirit and how He helps you? Read John 14:26 and Acts 2:38.

Does God Really Love Me...Always?

Can you finish this sentence?

I feel loved when _____
_____.

Hmmm. I wonder what you wrote. I will tell you mine—I feel loved when someone buys me a present!

Maybe you feel loved when you get a really good grade, score the winning goal, or when your mom snuggles with you and gives you a really big hug. Or maybe it's when someone you love gives you a smile.

All of these are really great things and can definitely make you feel special on the inside.

When you feel loved, you are probably kinder to others, you feel safer, happy, and want to do your best. Sometimes you may even feel like you have to keep working hard at being kind to make sure you are always loved.

Now, can I ask you another question? This one may be a little harder to answer, but I think you can handle it, okay?

When *don't* you feel loved?

That's more difficult to think about, right?

Well, you don't have to tell anyone what you answered to either of these questions, but here is what you need to know: "The LORD is good and his love endures forever; his faithfulness continues through all generations" (Psalm 100:5).

In case you are wondering, Yahweh means "God" in Hebrew. So in other words, this Scripture is saying God loves you forever.

Yes, forever!

God wants you to know that no matter what you may feel like, you are loved, and not just today but forever! You may have a lot of people around who love you, but no one's love for you is as special as God's.

Wow—that is fantastic news, isn't it? This means you can always feel safe and happy. And when you feel safe and happy you are most likely willing to do your best! Knowing this should also help you to be kind to those around you, with the same kindness God has shown you.

Now, I want you to know there are times when you may feel sad or disappointed, and God loves you then too. Even when you do not feel your best, remember that you are still loved. Even when you fail, God loves you! And when you feel like you have to work harder to be loved, well, God already loves you more than you'll ever know, and you don't have to do anything to earn His love.

Romans 8:39 reminds us that "neither height nor depth, nor anything else in all creation, will be able to separate us from the love of God that is in Christ Jesus our Lord."

You heard it! Nothing at all. His love is here to stay.

Dear God, thank You for loving me. I am so glad to know that You love me today and that You will love me forever! When I am sad and even when I feel my best, will You remind me of Your love for me? I pray that You will teach me how to show Your love to others around me. In Jesus's name, amen.

Fill in your name in this Scripture, John 3:16, to remind yourself how much God loves you! Remember that the Bible is not just God's Word; it is God's Word to *you*!

God so loved _____

that he gave his one and only Son, that [if]

_____ *believes in him*

[she] shall not perish but have eternal life.

What Else Does God Want from Me?

I love science museums. I don't think you have to be a scientist to enjoy creating a strange invention or to try an interesting experiment. A science museum is the perfect place for me and all not-so-scientific people to have a great time. There are always really cool and fascinating things to do and see.

For example, I once saw a robot contest! The robots were not competing against each other, but the robot's inventors were. *Inventor* is just a big word for a creator of things.

Several different people had designed some pretty interesting robots. Some of the robots could pick up things, turn into cars, and even respond to a question they had been asked. Do you know what else? All the robots' inventors were only about 12 years old!

Everyone watching was so impressed with what the inventors were able to make their robots do. After all, a robot is only good when it does exactly what it is told.

Robots do not have hearts, emotions, or brains. It would be a disaster if robots started making their own choices and doing whatever they wanted. They would have no way of knowing what was right or wrong, what hurt others, or even what hurt them. Because they do not have feelings, they don't know what it feels like to have joy or to be sad. Robots are created for obedience only.

While I watched those amazing robots follow all the rules they had been given, do you know what made me the happiest? I was really happy that I was not one of them! I am so grateful that God did not want me to be a robot.

Sometimes it may feel like loving God means you just have to follow rules, but that is not true! God doesn't want robots. If He wanted someone to just follow rules because someone told them to, then He would not have created people!

Yes, your obedience matters a lot and God definitely expects you to do what He says. But even more than that, He wants you to want to obey Him because of how much you love Him. He wants your heart.

When you love someone, you enjoy making them happy and you want to do what they ask you to do, right? Well, this is exactly what God wants from us.

Proverbs 23:26 says, "Give me your heart and let your eyes delight in my ways."

Giving God our hearts is the most important step of obedience. After that, He shows you and teaches you what He has for you to do. God wants you to love Him with your heart and your actions.

Dear God, thank You for not making me a robot. I am so glad I know what it feels like to have a heart and feelings! Help me to be obedient, and I pray that You will show me the joy that loving and choosing You brings. In Jesus's name, amen.

 Here are two Scriptures to help you as you love God with your heart and your actions. Write these down on a notecard and put it in a place you can see every day.

Philippians 2:14

1 Thessalonians 5:16-18

Why Is She So Perfect?

She was beautiful. She had long legs, dark wavy hair, a big smile, perfect teeth, and a contagious personality. She was also very funny, nice to everyone, not shy at all, and got straight A's. In other words, she was the girl everyone else wanted to be friends with! You know those kinds of girls, don't you?

Well, she was my friend!

I loved having her as my friend, but sometimes it made me a little sad because we were total opposites. I had short legs and was always too shy to be funny, and that made people think I was mean even though I really wasn't! I did have pretty good grades and a nice smile, but honestly, sometimes it was really hard to be her friend because I wanted to be more like her. I didn't want to be shy and I wanted people to want to be my friend too.

But it felt like people enjoyed being with her way more than they enjoyed being with me and that they valued her friendship more.

I knew it wasn't true but sometimes it made me feel a little worthless.

Have you ever felt like this?

It can be really hard not to compare yourself to the people who are closest to you—like your sisters, cousins, or even your best friend.

Believe it or not, the person you think you want to be more like probably has things she wishes she could change about herself too!

Comparing yourself to others is a pretty dangerous thing. I am sure you never feel good after you think about all the things you wish were different, do you? Comparing yourself to others can make you feel less special, less important, and less valuable.

What you need to remember is being different from someone else does not make you any less valuable.

It's actually the opposite! Your differences are gifts from God and they are exactly what make you both so special. God created you just the way you are and gave you the personality, looks, and talents He wanted you to have because He has things He wants you to do!

You are valuable to God.

Luke 12:7 says: "The very hairs of your head are all numbered. Don't be afraid; you are worth more than many sparrows."

Do you know what a sparrow is? It is a type of bird. When Jesus lived on earth, you could buy two sparrows for one penny! They were really cheap and people probably didn't value them as much as they valued other animals or even other foods.

So if God values sparrows, how much do you think He values you! The next time you start to compare yourself to someone else, choose to celebrate what makes you different from the person you're thinking about instead. Be grateful for the special way God has made you and your friends, because you're worth so much to Him just the way you are!

Dear God, thank You for giving me friends who are so special. I am grateful that You made each of us so different. Sometimes it is hard not to want to be like others because I think they are so great! Will You help me to realize how special I am too? Help me to know that just because I am different does not make me any less valuable than anyone else.

Think about your best friend. Make a list of all the great things about her and write a letter letting her know how great you think she is!

What If I Fail?

What would you do if you knew you could not fail? That means you would never be disappointed and you would always win!

Have you ever thought about that?

Would you try out for the volleyball team? Run for class president? Or even learn a new trick on your skateboard?

Would you start a conversation with the girl you think is really cool if you knew she would love talking to you? Or maybe you would raise your hand more often in class to answer a question if you knew you'd be right every time? That would be great, wouldn't it?

Unfortunately, sometimes our answers are wrong, we lose volleyball games, and the people we want to talk to don't always want to talk to us.

I know failure does not feel good. However, you should not let the fear of failing stop you from trying something new or doing something challenging.

Did you know the Bible says that with God's help you can do anything?

Philippians 4:13 says, "I can do all this through him who gives me strength."

That is good news, right? But let's think for a second. I don't want you to get the wrong idea.

The type of success God promises does not mean you will make every soccer goal, always answer a question right, and ride a skateboard better than anyone you know. The truth is, even as His child you may never do any of those things.

When God says you can do all things, He means that no matter what happens, He will give you the strength you need to handle it. If you lose or if you win, or if you fall, fail, or mess up, God is with you and will help you move forward with your life.

In other words, do not let the fear of disappointment scare you! God will help you and wants to use everything about your life to teach you and others more about Him.

Knowing this actually means you are a winner even if you lose!

Paul was one of Jesus's followers, and he experienced a lot of good and bad things. He even went to jail for loving and following Jesus. But Paul continued to do things that challenged him because he knew no matter what, God was always with him.

Don't be afraid to try things. Just as He was for Paul, God is with you! With Him and His love, you can never really fail.

Dear God, I am so glad to know You are with me and that with You I can do all things! Help me to trust that even if I fail, You will walk with me through it and remind me that I'm still winning. Also help me to be grateful when I win and to always share Your love in every situation.

Has God ever helped you do something you were really afraid to do? Maybe you did it and it was great or maybe it wasn't great and God helped you through it. Describe what happened and how God showed you that you really can do all things!

Why Can't I Just Be like Everyone Else?

Animals have some really strange names, don't they? Names like elk, penguin, gorilla, zebra, and buffalo! They certainly sound funny, and the more you say them, the funnier they sound.

Sometimes I like to think about how an animal may have gotten their name. Maybe it's because they were mixed with another animal and their two names were put together. Like a wholphin, which is a rare mix of a whale and a dolphin! Or maybe some animals' names were chosen because of where they are from or the type of food they like. For example, I bet you can guess what an anteater eats, right?

There are so many different animals and so many different names!

Can you think of an animal whose name makes total sense?

I know one! Have you ever heard of a ghost crab?

Imagine what that looks like...and you are probably right!

A ghost crab is a crab that looks ghostly! It is the same color as sand, which makes it seem invisible. They can also pull their dark eyes in really close to their bodies so sometimes all you see are little black circles.

Ghost crabs do not really bother people and they do not cause any trouble because, well, no one really even sees them! If you were walking on the beach in Brazil, they would probably surround you without you even knowing it. They mostly come out at night and some people like to watch for them on the beach after dark.

Well, being a ghost crab may sound pretty cool, but if you think about it, it's probably not that great. If you blend right in with everything around you, then others have a hard time seeing how fascinating and fantastic you are!

Have you ever wanted to be invisible? Maybe it feels like it would be easier to make friends if you just blended right in. Like a ghost crab, you would never disturb anyone or make anyone upset.

But God did not create you to be like a ghost crab! He made you to stand out and look different from everyone else around you. He doesn't want you to just go along with what is happening around you.

Romans 12:2 says, "Do not conform to the pattern of this world, but be transformed by the renewing of your mind. Then you will be able to test and approve what God's will is—his good, pleasing and perfect will."

God wants people to see you as His child so they can see Him!

Yes, you may look like your sister and you may have the same nose as your mom, but that's not exactly what I am talking about.

God created His children to stand out with their actions. He created you to be different, bright, and full of Him.

Dear God, help me to stand out, not so people will see me but so they will see You! I want to look and act different from what is around me. I pray that when people are looking for You, they can see the difference You make in me. In Jesus's name, amen.

Celebrate You!

Now that you know how special you are on the inside, do you know that it is okay to have a little fun and celebrate the unique way God made you look on the outside too?

Your hair can be one of the most unique things about you. Here are three tips to help you enjoy and appreciate your hair! When you're having a bad hair day...

1. **Accessorize!** You can braid different color ribbons together, add flowers to headbands, or even use shoestring or yarn. Just be creative and let your hair be just as unique as your personality!

2. **Have fun with your hair!** Don't be afraid to try new styles. After all, it's only hair. Once you have permission from your mom, have fun and be creative with your styles and hair accessories.

3. **Do *not* scream or complain while getting your hair done!** Be patient with your mom (or whoever does your hair). You know you will like it in the end.

Why Can't I Say Whatever I Want?

I have never broken any bones in my body and I am so thankful for that. I imagine it hurts pretty bad and I really don't think I would be able to handle it!

I don't like pain very much at all. I am actually a big baby about it! Sometimes I want to cry just from biting my tongue. A tongue is such a small part of your body, but biting it is one of the most painful things you can do.

Ouch!

I am sure you have bitten your tongue before, right? So you know exactly what I mean!

I imagine you were in the middle of eating something delicious—like a chocolate chip cookie or a nice big piece of steak! Mmmmm. You were just chewing and chewing, probably really fast and not really paying attention, when all of a sudden you felt the pain.

Have you ever "bitten your tongue" when you weren't even eating or chewing? "Bite your tongue" can also be a way of saying, "Choose to be quiet."

Ouch! That can be painful too!

For example, your sister is doing her homework and you can tell she is not in a good mood. You ask her a question and her response is not very kind. Your brain begins to fill up with all the mean things you can say back to her and you are ready to argue. However, just when you are about to open your mouth—you choose not to.

Or maybe your mother tells you to help clean up the playroom and you think of all the reasons you should not have to do it. Instead of giving those reasons to your mom, you quietly go into the room and do what she asked you to do.

This type of biting your tongue is not an accident; it is a choice. And it is a choice God wants you to make.

Choosing to be quiet, or choosing to "bite your tongue," can be hard, and it does not always feel good. It is not easy to keep words inside of us when we really want to say them! But when the words you want to say are harmful to someone or not helpful to a situation, then biting your tongue is the best thing you can do.

Of course, God can help, and He wants to! He will help you "bite your tongue." Psalm 141:3 says, "Set a guard over my mouth, LORD; keep watch over the door of my lips."

If you are like me and have a hard time handling the pain of biting your tongue, choosing to keep quiet, then this is the perfect prayer for you! Memorize it, and instead of letting mean and hurtful words come out of your mouth, choose to say this instead.

Dear God, You know everything about me and You are always ready to help me make better choices. Will You help me to choose to be quiet no matter how hard it is or how painful it may feel? I do not need to say everything I want to say and I pray You will guard my mouth and teach me to "bite my tongue"!

Do you have words that you need to get out? Try writing them down! The next time you choose to "bite your tongue," find a piece of paper and write down what you wanted to say. Now, after you write it, pray and ask God to clean your heart and your mind of hurtful words, then ball up that paper and throw it in the trash! Writing the words may help you to get them out, but you do not need to keep them or focus on them. Give them to God instead.

What Am I Saying?

Communication is a big word, but it's really not that fancy or hard to understand. You may not say the word *communication* often, but I am positive that you communicate every day. Don't you? You communicate with your family, your friends, and even your dog!

Communication is the way you connect with or deliver messages to the other living beings around you.

So how exactly do you do this communication thing?

Well, God gave us so many wonderful ways!

Of course, words are the most popular way to communicate. Actually, you speak between seven and twenty thousand words every day! But do you think it is possible to deliver messages to people without ever saying a word?

Absolutely! And guess what! We all do it. You are delivering messages all day even if you never say a word.

When you smile, nod your head, wave your hands, or put a frown on your face, you are communicating with others.

Even when you send a message on an electronic device full of emoticons (you know, all the little symbols, shapes, and characters) and no words, you are still saying a lot!

So although words are definitely a special way people communicate, we connect with those around us in so many other ways.

Unfortunately, I think we forget how many of the things we do, like it or not, deliver a message to those around us.

For example, do the faces you make and the way you sit, stand, or hold your head all deliver the message you want, to the people watching?

Often we do not think about what our body is saying to the people around us.

I want you to think about it. When you are in class, if you sit up straight and smile at your teacher, what message are you delivering?

If you slouch in your chair, cross your arms, and lay your head on your desk, what do you think you are saying to your teacher?

How do you think these different messages make your teacher feel?

Psalm 19:14 says, "May these words of my mouth and this meditation of my heart be pleasing in your sight, LORD, my Rock and my Redeemer."

What is happening in your heart plays a big part in the messages you deliver. God wants you to honor Him with all the ways He has given you to communicate, and He cares deeply about what is happening in your heart. If you find yourself using words or expressing yourself in a way you know God wouldn't appreciate, pray this verse above and ask God to give you the right words and the right thoughts in your heart.

Your words, body language, facial expressions, and even your text messages and emoticons should show God's love and a heart in love with Him!

Dear God, You have given me so many wonderful messages and You always teach me with Your Word. I pray You will help me to communicate Your love with others around me. Guide my words, my facial expressions, my body language, and all the other ways I communicate. Help my heart to be focused on and in love with You.

Create your own emoticons! If you had to go throughout your day without using words, what symbols would you use? Use this space to tell a story with symbols only!

Why Do Teenagers Get to Have All the Fun?

As a little girl, I was the youngest in my family. My brother was five years older than me and so were all of my cousins and his friends! They always hung out together and never thought I was old enough to do the things they were doing.

Have you ever wished you were a teenager, or maybe just older than you are?

Older kids look so cool, don't they? They always seem to be having fun with their friends. They get to stay up late, watch more television, drive, shop for their own clothes and shoes, and they get to wear makeup!

It all seems so fancy and fun! It's not fair, is it? Have you ever felt like you just can't wait until it's your turn?

Well, now that I am older, I know it is true that being a teenager can be fun, but I have learned that many perks we think come with being older are not really true. I think it's only fair to share some of those realities with you. Once you know the truth, you may start to see things a little differently.

You may think:

- Teenagers get to do whatever they want.
- Teenagers get to wear whatever they want.
- Teenagers can stay up late.

But the truth is:

- Teenagers still have to ask an adult for permission to

do things and they have to follow instructions and be obedient.

- The Bible tells us it's important to be modest in how we dress, no matter how old we are.

- Teenagers' bodies require more sleep than yours does! The problem is, they normally have a ton of schoolwork, chores around the house, and other responsibilities that interfere with them getting the sleep they really need!

So you see, being a teenager is not much different from being you! Being your age and being a teenager both have good things about them, but they both come with challenges too.

Here is what I want you to do: Be yourself today!

Everything happens at the time when it is supposed to. Don't rush today because you are in a big hurry to grow up. If you do that, then you may miss all the fun and fantastic things God has for you right now.

The Bible tells us God has plans for us, not just for later but for every day. His plans are good!

Jeremiah 29:11 says, "'I know the plans I have for you,' declares the LORD, 'plans to prosper you and not to harm you, plans to give you hope and a future.'"

Think about the friends you have made, the fun parties and celebrations you have had, and all the great things God is teaching you about Him. Would you want to skip any of that just so you can be older? I hope not!

Each age is special and every experience you have is all a part of God's plan. So keep living today and focus on growing closer to Jesus.

As you keep getting older, trust Him. He already has plans for you and wants to help you do the things He wants you to do!

Dear God, sometimes I want to grow up so much! Help me to trust that You have good plans for me, both now and later. Help me not to rush to grow up but to enjoy the life You have given me right now. I am grateful for the friends I get to grow with and memories I am making. I pray that I make wise decisions now so I can be responsible as I get older. In Jesus's name, amen.

 Now that you know being a teenager is not as easy as it looks, why don't you pray for the teenagers you know? Maybe you have an older sibling, older cousins, or someone in your neighborhood who is a teenager. Think of one or a few and pray these Scriptures for them.

- Read Numbers 6:24-26.
  Lord, I pray that You bless _____.

- Read Matthew 5:16.
  Lord, I pray that You help _____
  to be a leader and an example to her friends.

- Read Deuteronomy 31:6.
  Lord, I pray that _____
  knows You are with him.

- Read James 4:8.
  Lord, I pray that _____
  stays close to You.

Why Can't I Do Anything Right?

Sometimes growing up can be really difficult. It may feel like you are always doing something wrong or disappointing someone.

Being corrected is not fun, and I know it doesn't feel good when everything you do feels wrong or not good enough.

Maybe your mom is always correcting your attitude. Or maybe your teacher always corrects your answers. Does your coach correct how you kick the ball? Or does your Bible study teacher keep telling you all the things God wants you to do that you're not doing?

Does it ever feel like all you hear is, "Fix that" or "Change this"?

Has it ever made you just want to give up? After all, if you can't do things right, then why try at all? Right?

Wrong! Growing up is hard, but be patient and do not give up!

It may feel like you are always in trouble, but the truth is you are loved. Seriously!

Think about it. Would you take time to teach someone or discipline them if you did not care about them?

The only reason you want to see someone do better is that you love them so much and want what is best for them!

For example, if you have a pet, then I bet you take time to train him not to run into the street and to stay close to you. You correct him if he does not do it. Not because you are being mean to him, but because you love him and you don't want him to get hit by a car!

The same is true for you. God does not want to see you fail. He wants to teach you so you have the best life. That means learning and trusting that He is doing what is best for you. Sometimes He uses your parents, your teachers, and even your friends to challenge you to do better.

He also uses the Bible.

God wants you to know He sees you, knows you, and loves you. His love is the reason He corrects you.

Sounds crazy, but it's so true. Proverbs 3:12 says, "The LORD disciplines those he loves, as a father the son he delights in."

As you keep getting older, always be willing to learn and accept correction. If it is coming from God, then you know it is actually love.

Ask God to help you have a heart willing to listen to Him. Also pray that He will surround you with people who love Him and want to see you grow in His love!

Dear God, sometimes it feels like I am always in trouble. Help me to be patient and to remember that I am loved even when I am not doing everything right. I pray that You will give me a heart that is always willing to listen and willing to be obedient to You. Thank You for loving me. In Jesus's name, amen.

You are not the only one who doesn't do everything right. None of us do! Just remember that God's love for you is big and you are not alone.

Do you know the story of Jonah? Read Jonah 1–4. If that seems like a lot, read one chapter a night for the next four nights. Why don't you invite your mom, dad, or sibling to read it with you each night?

You will see that Jonah is very disobedient, but you will also see how God continues to show Jonah love as He disciplines and teaches him.

Wynter Pitts is the founder of For Girls Like You—
a ministry to girls that includes a print magazine—
and the niece of Dr. Tony Evans. She has a drive to
introduce young girls to Christian values so they can
walk passionately and boldly. A native of Baltimore,
Wynter resides in Dallas, Texas, with her husband, Jonathan, and their four daughters.

To learn more about books by Wynter Pitts
or to read sample chapters, visit our website at
www.harvesthousepublishers.com

For Girls Like You

For Girls Like You is a ministry to young girls and their parents that also includes a quarterly print magazine, journal, and other print and web resources. We have a passion and drive to introduce young girls to Christian values in a way that they are able to understand and digest so they can walk passionately and boldly in who God has created them to be.

We are dedicated to exposing girls to all the things they love (travel, positive role models, creative projects, etc.) without the negative messages, imagery, and advertising that often appear in mainstream entertainment. Instead we want every article, interview, and photo to support a Christ-centered system for our young girls!

Each issue of *For Girls Like You* is fun and colorful, featuring contributions and interviews from familiar faces as well as everyday girls who are choosing to live and shine for Christ. From designing clothing to researching biblical principles, this magazine supports parents' efforts to raise beautiful and healthy daughters whose identity is wrapped up in the love of Jesus.

For more information or to subscribe to the magazine, visit
www.forgirlslikeyou.com.